"Building relationships with our nei[ ] communities, better cities, and ultimately . . . a better world. Dave and Jay have written a powerful primer on neighboring. I encourage you to read this book and to step outside your front door and start making a difference."

Ken Blanchard, co-author of *The One Minute Manager®* and *Lead Like Jesus*

"*The Art of Neighboring* is a tool that is helping government and faith-based leaders work together to serve their communities. That by itself would be enough to recommend it. But it does more. It encourages people of faith to live as Jesus intended."

Reggie McNeal, missional leadership specialist for Leadership Network

"The Great Commandment of Jesus is not optional. Jay and Dave hold readers accountable to live out the Great Commandment in literal and creative ways. *The Art of Neighboring* is a unique and necessary addition to any serious Christian's missional library."

Ed Stetzer, president of LifeWay Research and author of *Subversive Kingdom*

"*The Art of Neighboring* is at the forefront of a national movement to renew local communities. This book explains why neighboring really matters and reminds us all of the value of pursuing relationships with the people who live around us."

John McKnight, co-director of the Asset-Based Community Development Institute, Northwestern University

"Jay Pathak and Dave Runyon provide thought-provoking yet practical insights on what it means to love your neighbor. The truths in the book have the potential to transform not only your life but also your entire community. This is a book you can't afford to miss."

Margaret Feinberg, author of *Scouting the Divine* and *The Sacred Echo*

"I live in the same city as Dave and Jay, and I can tell you that they are the real deal. If you are tired of living at a hectic pace and just skimming the surface of life . . . then stop everything you're doing and take the art of neighboring as seriously as Jesus did. This story is the essence of Christianity and has the potential to change everything!"

Hugh Halter, author of *The Tangible Kingdom* and *Sacrilege*

"If you dare follow Jay and Dave into this great adventure of neighboring, your lives and your neighborhoods will never be the same."

Carl Medearis, author of *Speaking of Jesus*

"The act of loving our actual neighbors is one of the simplest and yet most powerful things that we can do to make an impact in our world. I have seen the model described in this book close up, and it is the real deal. If you care about your city, if you long to see the fabric of your community change for the better, then you need to read this book."

Eric Swanson, co-author of *To Transform a City*

"I've always wondered how the churches in our city could work together to impact our community in a significant way. *The Art of Neighboring* has united many of the churches in Duluth and has helped us to launch a neighboring movement. I'm excited about the influence that *The Art of Neighboring* is having in our city and its potential to impact other cities around the country."

Don Ness, mayor of Duluth, MN

The Art of Neighboring

Building Genuine Relationships
Right Outside Your Door

Jay Pathak and Dave Runyon

BakerBooks

a division of Baker Publishing Group
Grand Rapids, Michigan

Published by Baker Books
a division of Baker Publishing Group
P.O. Box 6287, Grand Rapids, MI 49516-6287
www.bakerbooks.com

Printed in the United States of America

Library of Congress Cataloging-in-Publication Data
Pathak, Jay, 1976–
    The art of neighboring : building genuine relationships right outside your door / Jay Pathak and Dave Runyon.
        p.   cm.
    Includes bibliographical references (p.   ).
    ISBN 978-0-8010-1459-8 (pbk.)
    1. Evangelistic work. 2. Neighborliness—Religious aspects—Christianity.
I. Runyon, Dave, 1974– II. Title.
BV3793.P33 2012
248′.5—dc23   2012010197

Published in association with the literary agency of WordServe Literary Group, Ltd., www.wordserveliterary.com.

16 17 18 19 20   14 13

To Danielle and Lauren, our wives,
and the best neighbors we know

Contents

Foreword

One of my favorite shows is HGTV's *House Hunters*. It's a reality show that follows people who are searching for a place to live. If you watch the show, you will notice that when looking for a new home, almost everyone focuses on what's on the inside and outside of the house itself. Does the kitchen have granite countertops? Is there a finished basement? Does the front of the house have good curb appeal? Is the house located in a solid school district?

But one question I have never heard asked is, Who are the neighbors?

This is surprising to me because the individuals we live next to have a big impact on the quality of our lives. In the grand scheme of things, relationships are much more important than bricks and mortar, and our neighborhoods are much more than collections of houses.

Our family has lived in five neighborhoods over the last thirty years. Shortly after our third move, God opened my eyes to the value of neighboring. As a result, my wife and I felt God calling us to make it a priority to get to know the people who lived around us. This has been a life-changing decision for our entire family.

As we began to reach out to our neighbors, we quickly discovered that the benefits were far-reaching. We ended up being cared for by our neighbors as much as, if not more than, we cared for them. We began to experience what it's like to have a strong support system right outside our front door. We all have a need for genuine community, and nothing beats the frequency, availability, and spontaneity of connecting deeply with others who live nearby.

I also learned that the story of Jesus becomes evident whenever we connect with the people who live closest to us. Jesus said, "Everyone will know that you are my disciples, if you love one another" (John 13:35). The practice of neighboring creates incredible opportunities for us as believers to connect our story to the stories of our neighbors and to God's story.

We lived in that neighborhood for seven years before God called us to our next adventure. Our house didn't have granite countertops or stainless steel appliances. However, it became our "dream home" because of the relationships that we developed with our neighbors. Our street was filled with people who knew and cared for one another. As I learned to make time to be intentional in my neighborhood, I began to live at a healthier pace.

I first heard about the Denver Neighboring movement a few years ago through a close friend of mine. He shared a story about a group of pastors who had been challenged to launch a neighboring movement by their local government leaders. As I learned more about their story, I became intrigued and excited about what God was doing in their midst. I have always felt that if local congregations could work together on this issue, then great things were bound to happen. Adding civic leaders to the mix is icing on the cake. This is the type of movement that has the potential to change individuals, neighborhoods, and even entire cities.

Dave Runyon and I have become friends and golfing buddies as a result of our shared passion to encourage believers to become great neighbors. After reading this book, it is clear to me that he and Jay Pathak are two of the emerging leaders in the new neighboring movement that is gaining momentum across the country. Together they have written a powerful book that provides practical advice on how to be intentional about living out the Great Commandment. Their challenge is one that every Christian needs to hear and take to heart.

I am convinced that living in close community with our neighbors is the best way to live. The command to love our neighbors lies at the core of God's plan for our lives, and when we follow this mandate, it changes everything. The journey begins when we choose a lifestyle of conversation and community over a lifestyle of busyness and accumulation. It's about making room for life and choosing to befriend those God has placed around us.

Over the last thirty years I have had the privilege and opportunity to serve in several large churches and to speak all around the world. After years of doing ministry, I am more convinced than ever that we need practical ways to reach into the lives of those who are all around us. Large gatherings and great programs won't necessarily engage the people in our communities who don't know God. But neighboring will. There is a huge need today for simple and effective tools to encourage followers of Jesus to become better neighbors. What I love about this book is that Dave and Jay provide practical tools to help us all become the neighbors God wants us to be.

The Art of Neighboring invites us to step into the kind of relationships and life rhythms we were created to enjoy. This book is much more than a book about neighboring. In the pages that follow, Dave and Jay describe a simple yet profoundly meaningful way to live.

It is my hope and desire that the message in this book will be embraced and lived out by leaders, pastors, and believers everywhere!

Randy Frazee, author of *Making Room for Life* and *The Connecting Church*; senior minister, Oak Hills Church, San Antonio

Acknowledgments

Many of the people who know us well laughed openly when we told them we were writing a book. There were others, however, who encouraged us along the way, and we would like to acknowledge them.

First and foremost, we are grateful for the pastors in our local network in Arvada. You have been a significant part of this story, and we are excited to see what the future holds. We also want to acknowledge the local government leaders in our community, specifically, Bob and Candy Frie, Vicky Reier, and Don Wick. Thank you for being an incredible resource along the way.

A number of people have served as mentors and friends throughout this process. Thank you to Dan Thoemke, Eric Swanson, Pete Richardson, Carl Medearis, Hugh Halter, Jim Herrington, Randy Frazee, Rich Nathan, Gary Poole, Howard

Lawrence, Mike McFadden, Pat Runyon, and Don Reeverts. Additionally, we have been influenced by several city-reaching movements around the country, namely Mission Houston, Unite in Atlanta, Vision San Diego, and Christ Together in Chicago.

We also want to thank the staff and people at the Mile High Vineyard, Foothills Community Church, as well as Benson, Kerrane, Storz & Nelson. All of you have been a critical part of the journey.

This book wouldn't have been written if it weren't for our agent, Greg Johnson, and his insistence that we write this story. We are grateful for the hard work of Marcus Brotherton, who spent tireless hours compiling our thoughts and putting them on paper. We are indebted to Heather Mundt and Leif Oines for helping to fine-tune the final manuscript. We are still amazed that Jon Wilcox and the rest of the team at Baker took a chance on the two of us. Thanks for rolling the dice. Also, thanks to Wes and Allyson Gardner and Doug and Catherine Benson for believing in us and making all of this possible!

It would be impossible to acknowledge properly everyone who has contributed to this book. There have been so many who have poured so much into us over the course of our lives. There is very little in this book that hasn't been said by others first. We are grateful for all of those who have come before us.

Last but not least, we want to thank our neighbors. You have taught us more than you will ever know.

1

Who Is My Neighbor?

What if the solution to our society's biggest issues has been right under our noses for the past two thousand years? When Jesus was asked to reduce everything in the Bible into one command he said: Love God with everything you have *and* love your neighbor as yourself. What if he meant that we should love our *actual* neighbors? You know, the people who live right next door.

The problem is that we have turned this simple idea into a nice saying. We put it on bumper stickers and T-shirts and go on with our lives without actually putting it into practice. But the fact is, Jesus has given us a practical plan that we *can* actually put into practice, a plan that has the potential to change the world. The reality is, though, that the majority of Christians don't even know the names of most of their neighbors.

We know that getting to know your neighbors can sometimes be intimidating. If you're like us, when you watch the news you can't help but feel overwhelmed. There are endless stories of child abuse, drug and alcohol addiction, teen pregnancy, out-of-control debt, and a laundry list of other issues. Not only does it make you want to turn the channel and escape, but it also makes you wary of strangers, even the ones that live on your block.

We know this isn't the way it is supposed to be. This isn't what Jesus envisioned for us and for our world. We know we can do more. And we know that we can't just sit around waiting for someone else to do it. But it's hard to know where to start. Right?

Start by looking around your own neighborhood. What problems do you see? The yard across the street is full of knee-high weeds. You know the husband just got laid off from work. Should you call code enforcement? Maybe the local government will be the one to help.

Next door there are teenagers, and the smell of pot seeps out the windows on a nightly basis. You wonder if you should call the police. That will take care of the problem. Won't it?

There's a family a couple of doors down with several children. It's clear that none of them speak English very well, and you wonder if the kids are even in school. Should you contact someone in the school district? Surely they are equipped to handle this sort of problem. Aren't they?

These problems aren't hypothetical; they likely exist just outside your front door. We can always hope that somebody else will handle them. But what if we *could* be part of the solution? And what if the solution is more attainable than we think? What if it all starts with getting to know the invisible neighbors that surround us?

Have you ever wondered about the invisible family that lives in your neighborhood? You've never actually met them but you know they exist because you've glimpsed signs of life around their house.

There's the dad. You know him by the sedan he drives. When his garage door opens at 7:30 each morning, he's already inside his car. The motor starts. He backs out of the driveway and takes off down the street. Each evening he zooms straight into the garage again. The garage door opens and then shuts, and he's inside the house without a trace.

Then there's the mom. All you've glimpsed of her recently is her minivan. She zips their kids around to a mass of activities, probably going to soccer, karate, violin lessons, and playdates. You know about these activities mostly because of the different uniforms that the kids are wearing as they pile into the car. The stick-figure decal on the window is also helpful, a kind of suburban map legend on the rear window that tells the neighbors how many kids the family has and what they like to do.

Their kids always seem to hang out in the backseat. You can't really see much of them because the windows are tinted. But you can see the glow of the dual DVD players as the van passes, so you know they're in there.

And what about the three middle-aged adults who live in the house on the corner? What's their relationship, and why do they share the same house? And who lives across the street? There never seem to be any grown-ups around—only teenagers coming and going at all hours and playing their music really loudly. And why do the folks catty-corner leave their garbage cans by the curb for days? Do they travel a lot?

It's so easy to draw negative conclusions about the neighbors we've only glimpsed. An unkempt yard, a slew of tattoos, a weird haircut, or loud music. It can all cause us to make assumptions about the people who live around us. But it's these very assumptions that keep us from befriending them.

What if things could be different, though? What if we took the time to get to know the people next to us and discovered that they aren't so menacing after all? Perhaps we'd find that the people on our block are normal people just like us. They go to work, hang out with their kids, and put their pants on one leg at a time. At the end of the day, they long for a place to belong, a place to be accepted and cared for. They want to do something significant with their lives, something that really matters.

What good things might happen if you truly got to know the people in your neighborhood and they got to know you?

An Unexpected Messenger

In 2009 I (Dave) gathered a group of twenty lead pastors in the Denver area so we could think, dream, and pray about how our churches might join forces to serve our community. We invited our local mayor, Bob Frie, to join us, and we asked him a simple question: How can we as churches best work together to serve our city?

The ensuing discussion revealed a laundry list of social problems similar to what many cities face: at-risk kids, areas with dilapidated housing, child hunger, drug and alcohol abuse, loneliness, elderly shut-ins with no one to look in on them. The list went on and on.

Then the mayor said something that inspired our joint-church movement: "The majority of the issues that our community is facing would be eliminated or drastically reduced if *we could just figure out a way to become a community of great neighbors.*"

Later he explained that often when people identify a problem, they come to civic officials and say something like, "This is becoming a serious issue, and you should start a program to address it." Frie shared candidly with us that, in his opinion, government programs aren't always the most effective way to address social issues. He went on to say that relationships are more effective than programs because they are organic and ongoing. The idea is that when neighbors are in relationship with one another, the elderly shut-in gets cared for by the person next door, the at-risk kid gets mentored by a dad who lives on the block, and so on.

After the mayor left the meeting that day, our group of pastors was left to reflect on what he had shared. I (Jay) can remember sitting there, and before I could think, I just blurted out, "Am I the only one here who is a little bit embarrassed? I mean, here we were asking the mayor how we can best serve the city, and he basically tells us that it would be great if we could just get our people to obey the second half of the Great Commandment." In a word, the mayor invited a roomful of pastors to get their people to actually *obey* Jesus.

You know the Great Commandment, right? Love God with all your heart, mind, soul, and strength, and love your neighbor as yourself. It's a teaching found in Matthew 22:37–40 and repeated in the Bible for the purpose of reminding us how important it is. In Galatians 5:14 the apostle Paul says it most succinctly: "The entire law is summed up in a single command: 'Love your neighbor as yourself.'"

Love your neighbor as yourself. Could it be that simple? I (Dave) remember thinking, *Jesus is a genius! He is asked to pick one commandment that is more important than all the others. And he shares something that would change the world, if only every person who believes in Jesus would actually do it.*

The depth of the irony was not lost on those of us who were sitting in the room that day. God works in mysterious ways, and on that day he used a government official to urge a group of pastors to start a movement that was simple, powerful, and biblical.

Leaving that meeting, we began to pray about what God was leading us to do next. As we began to talk to other leaders in our city, we found that many of them shared the mayor's assessment. They saw that our neighborhoods were not as connected as they needed to be.

The next time we gathered, we invited Vicky Reier, the Arvada assistant city manager, to attend our meeting. We had heard her talk about neighboring in the past and we wanted to hear her thoughts on how to begin. As she talked about the reasons neighboring matters, Vicky said, "From the city's perspective, *there isn't a noticeable difference in how Christians and non-Christians neighbor in our community.*"

This was a moment that galvanized us. We realized something was wrong. We thought, *This isn't the way Jesus wanted it to be.* We had to do something!

As church leaders, we began to dream about what it would look like to start a neighboring movement among our people and in our city. We decided to come together and, with one voice, create a joint sermon series around the idea of taking the Great Commandment literally.

Each church in our network held a three-week teaching series following Easter Sunday. We developed a few resources for the churches to use, such as video interviews, sermon outlines, and illustrations.

Soon after the sermon series was launched, people responded and began taking steps to get to know their neighbors. Stories about block parties and new relationships began to pour in. City leaders began to talk about the initiative—as well as the value it created in their communities—all from people simply learning their neighbors' names and working with others to throw a block party. The results were immediate. New friendships evolved, strangers became acquaintances, and acquaintances began moving toward genuine relationships with one another.

By working together as churches, we drastically increased the scope of the initiative and quickly gained traction throughout our city. Such immediate results made us dream about how we could further connect the people in our twenty-plus congregations while encouraging them to continue making positive changes in their neighborhoods. We weren't concerened with getting people to connect with only those in their same church. Rather, we urged everyone to simply reach out and connect with kingdom-minded people willing to partner in their neighborhood. By working together in this manner, we were able to do things that we could never do alone.

The mayor was right. More importantly, Jesus was right. Neighboring relationships really do matter.

Taking the First Step

If you are anything like us, your head is spinning right about now. It's likely that your schedule is already packed and that the idea of becoming a good neighbor might sound impractical or even scary at first. But we invite you to lean into those issues. If you do, we are confident that you will discover that Jesus really is a genius. And that his master plan actually works.

The solutions to the problems in our neighborhoods aren't ultimately found in the government, police, or schools or in getting more people to go to church. The solutions lie with us. It's within our power to become good neighbors, to care for the people around us and to be cared for by the people around us. There really is a different way to live, and we are finding that it is actually the best way to live.

Often it's easy to take the teachings of Jesus and turn them into clichés. We're tempted to dial into these slogans whenever we're in crisis. But experience shows us that the slogans alone leave us hollow. So what would it look like to take the teachings of Jesus seriously and orient our daily lives around them? Let's be honest—we need to do a whole lot more than stick a fish symbol on the back of our car.

A Journey toward Neighboring

When I (Dave) was 26, I was hired as a teaching pastor at a large, young-adult church that was experiencing a lot of growth. In my previous life, I was a high school teacher. Then almost overnight, I went from teaching thirty kids in a classroom to talking in front of a couple thousand people. Needless to say, I was in way over my head.

We were supposedly one of the "hot" churches in town. Translation: this is where a bunch of "hot" people go to meet each other. (Incidentally, I met my beautiful wife at this church.) There was a lot of buzz surrounding what we were doing and how we were doing it. Local pastors would visit our church in hopes of discovering what it was that was prompting the growth and attracting so many young people.

Teaching in front of thousands of people felt like the opportunity of a lifetime. At least it did at first. And of course there were parts of my job that were exhilarating. On most nights, however, when I got into my car and drove home, I felt strangely empty. I knew what went into putting on those services. We spent the majority of our time putting on an event that, to be honest, just didn't seem like it was producing the kind of life change we were hoping to see.

My point is not to criticize large churches, because there are many good ones out there that are doing great things. Nor am I saying that large-group teaching isn't effective and that we should scrap it altogether. Instead I am saying that my experience as a large-church pastor caused me to reevaluate my thinking about transformation and the best ways to invest my time and energy. While I served there, a healthy sense of discontent grew in me. And over time I realized that our weekly service was always going to have a limited impact in actually changing our community. I became convinced that no matter how much our church grew, a single congregation would never be able to truly transform our entire city.

My healthy discontent sent me on a journey to redefine how I thought about the church and its ability to have a lasting impact. I left my teaching pastor position and found myself at another thriving church, where I continued to wrestle with the same gnawing thoughts and questions. I soon found myself becoming obsessed with John 17, an entire chapter that recounts Jesus's prayer just before he is arrested. First, Jesus prays for himself, then for his disciples. Then he concludes by praying for us.

What he prayed is powerful. He prayed that everyone who follows him would be one, that we would be brought to complete unity. Jesus has a burning desire for there to be unity among *all* believers. In fact, he tells us that there is something so sacred and beautiful about our oneness that it will draw people to God who aren't in a relationship with him. This was the answer I was looking for to help facilitate lasting transformation in our city! And this is what prompted me to gather local pastors to listen to our mayor and to dream about what we could do together that we could never do alone.

After hearing our mayor's comments about neighboring that day, I was forced to consider my own relationships with my literal neighbors. I came face-to-face with the fact that while I was doing a decent job caring for a lot of people in my church, I wasn't doing a good job of even remembering my neighbors' names. That conversation with our mayor launched my family on a journey of learning how to know and even love the people God has placed around us. As you will see throughout this book, this was a powerful turning point for my wife and me, and even for our kids. I have come to believe that, as followers of Jesus, one of the worthiest endeavors we can undertake is to take the Great Commandment seriously and learn to be in relationship with our literal neighbors.

We all need to get back to the basics of what he commanded: love God and love others. Everything else is secondary.

A Way That Works

Jesus said the most important thing we can do is to love God with all our heart, soul, mind, and strength, *and* to love our neighbor as ourselves. We are discovering that Jesus was actually really smart. You could even say that he was and is a genius. When Jesus was asked to reduce everything important into one command, he gave us a simple and powerful plan that, if acted on, would literally change the world.

This simple plan also offers us a different kind of life. It's a way of living that makes sense and brings peace to people's souls. Whenever we center our lives around the Great Commandment and take very literally the idea and practice of loving our neighbor, there's great freedom, peace, and depth of relationship that come to our lives. By becoming good neighbors, we become who we're supposed to be. As a result, our communities become the places that God intended them to be.

Relationships are progressive and don't all happen overnight, but there are some simple steps you can take that will start you on an amazing journey. Make no mistake, neighboring is not always easy. Yet it is powerful and significant. And it is central to experiencing the full life that Jesus promises.

2

Taking the Great
Commandment Seriously

A few years ago I (Jay) was on staff at a large church in the Midwest. Part of my job at that church was to create events to which people could invite their friends so they could hear about starting a new life with Jesus. I believed then, and I still do today, that Jesus has something good to offer people. And when they follow him, not only do they have eternal security, but the priorities of their lives are also rearranged for the better.

One of the events I planned was a concert. We booked a well-known band, got some radio time to promote the event, passed out flyers by the handful, and rented lights and smoke machines. I think we even had lasers. (You know it's a real concert if you've got lasers.) We planned for a couple thousand people to come. The night before the concert, I went to bed thinking, *This thing is gonna be huge.*

Shortly before the event was supposed to start I walked into the auditorium, and what I saw was disheartening. The entire audience consisted of about twenty-five people. That's right, twenty-five people.

I began to sweat, wondering what my next job would be after I got fired. Panicked, I got on my phone and started working through my contacts list. "You're bringing people, right? I don't care who it is. Just anybody. Force 'em into your car. Get 'em here!"

By the time the show started, a couple hundred people had shown up. But in a room where we were set up for a couple thousand, it was a painfully awkward night.

After the show, some friends and I went to a local dive to talk about what went wrong with our pathetic event. As we walked into the place right around the corner from the church, I realized it was jammed full of people. I asked the hostess, "Why's this place so full?"

"We just started this new thing a couple weeks ago," she said. "Every Thursday night we have a concert that draws a huge crowd."

At that moment, a lightbulb went on in my head. Just five minutes away from the building where I was desperately try-ing to gather a crowd, a crowd had already gathered. Maybe, I thought, just maybe, there's a way for *us* to go where the people already are, instead of trying to get people to come to us. I didn't figure out right away exactly how that concept might work, but it got me thinking.

It's common for churches to host big events and ask people

to invite their friends. This is not a bad thing and, in fact, has been an effective way for people to share their faith with friends and neighbors who don't know God. But at the same time, there are many people around us who will never attend one of these events. So it's important for us to think about how we can go to the places where they already are.

I think that most sincere followers of Jesus want to connect with people around them in a meaningful way, but often they just don't know how. And this raises some serious questions about our strategies to engage the world. Remember, Jesus talked about a way to be with people that is both effective and powerful, a way to be with them where they are.

A Simple Invitation

When Jesus said that all the commandments can be summed up in loving God and loving our neighbors, he was on to something. What would happen if we all just did what Jesus said to do? What if we get to know our actual neighbors? This sounds simple, but it's easy to miss.

So let's turn this around for a moment. Sometimes it's easier to see how *not* following the brilliance of Jesus can hurt us. Imagine what happens when people love each other well. Now imagine what happens when we *don't* love those who live next door. Odds are good that we will experience the following:

- *Isolation.* We will live lonely lives. It's far too easy to leave our house every morning with our head down. We grind it out at work, come back home, and hurry inside. We never get to know the people around us, and they don't get to know us.

- *Fear.* We will be wary of our neighbors, and they will be wary of us. Whatever is unknown is scary. So when we don't know our neighbors and they don't know us, it's easy to imagine the worst.

- *Misunderstanding.* When we don't know our neighbors, it's easy to get the wrong idea about one another. For instance, a friend of ours had a neighbor whose house was run down. The garage door was falling off the hinges. Two dead cars sat out front. So he called code enforcement, and officials came by and ticketed the house. A few days later he was talking to another neighbor about the blighted house. "Yeah," said the neighbor. "I guess the woman who lives in that home lives alone, and her mother has cancer. She had to stop working to care for her mom. She's been by her mom's bedside twenty-four hours a day for the past few months." You can imagine how horrible our friend felt once he got the full story.

Throughout the Bible, God tells us to love our neighbors. He emphasizes that along with loving him, this is the most important thing we can do. *God invites us to love the way he loves.* He challenges us to put our love into action.

The Implications of an Invitation

Not long after the concert fiasco, my wife, Danielle, and I were hosting a small group in our apartment. It had been a really long day, and I was exhausted. So as I was driving home, I called home and told my wife I wasn't sure that I could lead the group that night. She said, "Well, why don't we all just have dinner together? I'll call our group and ask them to bring food."

"Sounds great," I said. The thought appealed to me—an easy evening of relaxing with our small group and having dinner together. After all, that's what all small-group leaders do when they don't want to prep for the Bible study: host a last-minute potluck and call it "fellowship."

A funny thing, however, had happened by the time I arrived home. When I opened the door to our apartment, strangers were everywhere. They sat on my couch and wandered around in my kitchen. Strangers ate our food. There was even a stranger playing my guitar.

My guitar. My couch. My world was being invaded.

"Um, what's going on?" I asked Danielle.

"It's a party," she said cheerfully. "I thought it would be fun to invite some of our neighbors. Relax. Everyone's just grilling burgers, hanging out, and having a good time."

I confess that at first I wasn't thrilled with the idea. Okay, the truth is I was angry, mostly with my wife. Don't get me wrong. I love my wife and I loved that she so willingly invited these unknown neighbors into our home. But I work with people and their problems all day long. I wasn't sure I wanted more people invading my personal space. My job was simply to lead the small group, and I didn't feel like loving these other people, at least not now. As I looked around the room full of strangers, I found that I *needed to make a conscious effort to adjust my thinking to accommodate my neighbors.*

I needed to stop being selfish and be open to whatever was happening in that moment in my apartment.

Now I realize that long before that evening, I should have seen my tendency to be selfish. My life was becoming so crowded with helping people that I wasn't willing to help anyone "off the clock." And by "off the clock" I mean whenever I didn't want to. God was asking me to be flexible, and that's not easy for a schedule-oriented guy like me. But this is what happens when we come face-to-face with Jesus's invitation to love our neighbors.

The Good Samaritan

Maybe you've heard the story of the good Samaritan. It's found in Luke 10:25–37. One day, an expert in the law decided he wanted to test Jesus, so the man asked Jesus what he needed to do to inherit eternal life. Now, we imagine this law expert was a guy just like most folks we know: he preferred to hang out with people like himself. Undoubtedly he crammed his day full of activities and didn't want to find a house full of strangers when he came home in the evening.

Jesus turned the question back on the lawyer, making the lawyer answer his own question. "What is written in the Law? How do you read it?" Jesus asked him.

The expert in the law replied, "'Love the Lord your God with all your heart and with all your soul and with all your strength and with all your mind'; and, 'Love your neighbor as yourself.'" He knew the Bible well. He gave the right answer.

"Great," Jesus said. "Do this and you will live."

But the text goes on to give us great insight into this man's motives. It says, "But he wanted to justify himself, so he asked Jesus, 'And who is my neighbor?'"

It is important to note the statement "he wanted to justify himself." The man wanted to define this word *neighbor* in such a way that he could not be found blameworthy. If his *neighbor* was someone he could choose, then he'd be okay. By asking Jesus to define the word *neighbor*, this man was looking for a loophole.

Think about it: are we also trying to find a loophole in what Jesus said is the most important thing for us to live out? I (Jay) am amazed at my ability to do this. My first instinct is to make excuses, point out inconsistencies, and rationalize away the clear teaching of Jesus. We do this so naturally we don't even realize we're doing it. The lawyer's question and ours is, "Who is my neighbor?"

To answer the question, Jesus told the story of the good Samaritan.

A man was headed from Jerusalem to Jericho when he fell into the hands of robbers. They beat him badly, robbed him, and left him for dead. Though two religious leaders passed by on the road, they did not help the man. They were both people who prided themselves on doing the right thing, good religious folks, people who should have known better. But these two people had other things to do, schedules to keep, agendas that couldn't be flexed. And so they kept going. In Jesus's story the obvious point is that they failed the test.

Finally, a Samaritan stopped and helped the injured man. The Samaritan was from a culture known for hating Israelites, and the feeling was mutual. In the ears of Jesus's listeners, it would be the modern-day equivalent of a terrorist stopping to help him. Even so, Jesus said the Samaritan bandaged the man's wounds, loaded him on his donkey, and took him to an inn, the ancient equivalent of a hospital. The Samaritan even paid the man's medical bills. How's that for adjusting a schedule to help someone?

Jesus's point was that the Samaritan was actually the true neighbor. He told the expert in the law to "go and do likewise."

Who Is My Neighbor?

That's how neighboring starts in our hearts—we develop flexibility and compassion. But unfortunately we are often moving too fast to notice that those who are right around us need a good neighbor. We may not pass by an accident and have an opportunity to serve as a paramedic, but we are invited to adjust our schedules to accommodate those in need who are nearby. Perhaps the needs of our neighbors can be met simply by opening our home, grilling some hamburgers, and letting a guy sit on our couch and play our guitar. We can begin by noticing that we *have* neighbors, people who at the moment are nameless and faceless.

When we hear the story about the good Samaritan, we are tempted to fall into a trap similar to that of the expert in the law. He wanted to define who qualified as his neighbor. And in looking for a loophole, he missed the lesson Jesus tried to teach.

As we read this parable two thousand years later, it's tempting to turn the story of the good Samaritan into a metaphor.

If we're not careful, we can become numb to the power of the Great Commandment.

If we say, "Everyone is my neighbor," it can become an excuse for avoiding the implications of following the Great Commandment. Our "neighbors" become defined in the broadest of terms. They're the people across town, the people who are helped by the organizations that receive our donations, the people whom the government helps. We don't have to feel guilty, we tell ourselves. After all, we can't be expected to really love everybody, can we?

The problem is, however, that when we aim for everything, we hit nothing. So when we insist we're neighbors with everybody, often we end up being neighbors with nobody. That's our human nature. We become like the lawyer looking for a loophole. We tell ourselves that we've got a lot going on in our lives, so surely the Great Commandment applies only to the wounded enemy lying beside the road, doesn't it? Since we haven't come across many of those lately, surely we're doing just fine when it comes to loving our neighbors.

Maybe not.

Jesus assumed that his audience would be able to love those nearest to them, their literal neighbors, the people most like them, who shared the same heritage and geography. In telling the parable, Jesus was stretching their concept of neighbor to include even people from a group they didn't like.

Today as we read the parable, we go straight for loving the neighbor on the side of the road. Thus we make a metaphor of the neighbors——a metaphor that doesn't include the person who lives next door to us.

If we don't take Jesus's command literally, then we turn the Great Commandment into nothing more than a metaphor. We have a metaphoric love for our metaphoric neighbors, and our communities are changed—but only metaphorically, of course. In other words, nothing changes.

So in addition to thinking of our neighbor metaphorically, as did the good Samaritan, we need to apply Jesus's teaching to our literal neighbors—real people with real names, phone numbers, and addresses.

Where the Rubber Meets the Road

Let's try a quick exercise. Oh, and a warning. This might hurt a little bit.

We've both done this exercise with hundreds of churches and thousands of people, and a number of them have jokingly referred to this as "the chart of shame." This exercise might be convicting, and if it is, that's probably healthy. But the point of the exercise is not to bring shame; it's to move the Great Commandment from a theory into a real-world context.

To begin, imagine that the middle box in the chart on page 38 is your house and the other boxes are the eight houses situated nearest to you—the eight households that God has placed closest to where you live.

Now, you might live in a community that doesn't look like a tic-tac-toe board. That's okay. Whether you live on a greenbelt, a cul-de-sac, a rural lot with five-acre parcels, or in a corner apartment, try to picture the locations of your eight nearest neighbors—the eight who live closest to you—however they might be situated.

Then in the middle of the chart, simply write your home address. In the other boxes, fill in the three subpoints within each box—a, b, and c—as follows:

- a—Write the names of the people who live in the house represented by the box. If you can give first and last names, that's great. If it's only first names, that's fine too.

- b—Write down some relevant information about each person, some data or facts about him or her that you couldn't see just by standing in your driveway, things you might know if you've spoken to the person once or twice. We don't mean *drives a red car* or *has yellow roses by the sidewalk*, because you could see that from your driveway. We mean information you've gathered from actually speaking to a neighbor, such as *grew up in Idaho, is a lawyer, plays golf, is from Ethiopia, had a father in World War II.*

- c—Write down some in-depth information you would know after connecting with people. This might include their career plans or dreams of starting a family or anything to do with the purpose of their lives. What motivates them to do what they do? What would they say about God? What do they most fear? What are their spiritual beliefs and practices? Write down anything meaningful that you've learned through interacting with them.

a.

b.

c.

a.

b.

c.

a.

b.

c.

a.

b.

c.

a.

b.

c.

a.

b.

c.

a.

b.

c.

a.

b.

c.

Okay, how did you do? After leading this exercise numerous times in many different venues, we have observed that the results are strikingly consistent:

- About 10 percent of people can fill out the names of all eight of their neighbors, line a.
- About 3 percent can fill out line b for every home.
- Less than 1 percent can fill out line c for every home.

Take a step back and consider what this means. Jesus said to love our neighbors. Sure, the teaching extends to our metaphoric neighbors—people everywhere in need. This extends to the people we work with, the parent on our kid's soccer team, and even the person on the other side of the world who is in need of a meal. But it also means our *actual* neighbors—the people who live next door.

So are we doing this? Are we actually loving our neighbors? What does this exercise reveal about our neighboring or lack thereof? Our chart may not reveal what you'd like it to, and it's important not to shy away from how this makes you feel. Lean in and feel the burn.

Now let's take a minute to reconcile the reality of your chart with the Great Commandment. Jesus says that your enemy should be your neighbor. He says that you should go out of your way to be the neighbor of someone who comes from a place or history of open hostility toward you or your way of life. Clearly he's stretching our understanding of what it means to love. We would define this kind of love as advanced or graduate-level love. *The reality is that most of us aren't at the graduate level; we need to start with the basics.* We need to go back to kindergarten and think about our literal next-door neighbors before we attempt to love everyone else on the face of the planet. How could we begin, for example, to care for a wounded terrorist if we haven't reached out to our neighbors? So let's start by learning our neighbors' names. If you've lived next to your neighbors for a long time and still don't know their names, it can be awkward. But you have to start somewhere. They probably don't know your name either. Someone has to break the ice. Why not you?

And here's one more question to consider as you begin this journey: What do you think about when you hear the word *love*? Theologians write about it, poets muse about it, singers sing about it. We want to be really clear: we are none of those. We are relatively normal guys. We're not deep thinkers, nor do we have any musical skills whatsoever—we'd embarrass ourselves on a karaoke stage. And, if we happened to rhyme, it's not on purpose. But we do know this about love: to love someone, it helps to actually *know their name*.

The People Right Next Door

When I (Jay) came home that evening and found our apartment filled with strangers, it wasn't long before I realized I needed to adopt a better attitude. As the people in our small group began talking with our neighbors, a fascinating discussion ensued. One of the neighbors said, "You know, I've watched thirty people shuffle in and out of your apartment every week, and I've always wondered what all those people are doing."

Another noted, "Yeah, we hear music every week and laughing. And we've always thought we were missing out on something!"

It was at this unexpected gathering that Danielle and I began to discover who our neighbors really were. Strangers started becoming acquaintances, paving the way for genuine relationships. We didn't need to invite them to anything because they were already nearby. We just needed to open the door of our apartment and welcome them in.

Over the next few weeks, as we started to get to know our neighbors, some of them invited us into their lives. One man was struggling with addiction, and we started to help him walk in the direction of recovery. Another couple was on the verge of a divorce, so my wife and I became a sounding board for them as they worked through some of their issues. Many of the people were just regular folks, and we enjoyed their company. Slowly we began to care for the people in our apartment complex. It wasn't that we were professional counselors and had all the answers to everyone's problems. We simply started to get to know the people that God had placed around us. We started having real conversations with them and they with us.

Remember, it's easy to become numb to the Great Commandment. If we aren't careful, we can take the most important teaching of Jesus and turn it into a catchy saying that we don't live out. And in doing so, we become immune to its impact on our lives and the lives of others. We miss out on the life that Jesus has come to give us.

Remember the story of our friend who called code enforcement? The city came out and issued a ticket to the rundown house. When that man learned his neighbor's story, that his neighbor was spending every waking moment caring for her sick mother, he decided to do something. He rallied a few other neighbors, and they fixed the woman's garage door, hung up her gutters, and helped her fix her car. More important, they got to know her name and more of her story. In short, they let her know that she wasn't alone, that there were people nearby who cared. Simply knowing her story made all the difference.

We all agree that there are dozens of obstacles—some real, some imagined—that keep us from getting to know even one neighbor. Let's spend the next several chapters talking through those barriers and how we can overcome them.

3

The Time Barrier

The number-one obstacle to neighboring well is time. If you're taking the Great Commandment seriously, undoubtedly you will start to feel conflicted. You have relationships in your life already. And most of us aren't walking around with extra time, wondering what to do with it. We feel overwhelmed by the amount of stuff that is jammed into our schedules. Our lives are packed already. We already have enough relationships—how are we ever going to find time and energy for one more relationship, let alone six or seven or eight?

It's vital to take a step back and ask ourselves if we live at a pace that allows us to be available to those who live around us. That doesn't necessarily mean that you must stop everything you're doing right now. Instead it's about taking a look at your commitments and being willing to reprioritize to be more present with your close family and friends, as well as make space in your life for those living nearest to you.

The problem, though, is that we live in a world that values production, results, and activity. We tend to run from one task to another and then to another. Our in-boxes seem eternally full. There's always another voice mail to be returned or another email to write. Our to-do lists grow longer and longer even though we keep checking things off. Today we have more time-saving devices at our disposal than any generation in the history of the world, yet we feel as though we have less and less time to get things done. Who actually has time to stop and smell those proverbial roses anyway? How is this possible?

Think about it. Even fifteen years ago, you'd never have dreamed that in the near future you'd be able to:

- Make phone calls while riding in your car.
- Send mail electronically while riding in your car, while you are making phone calls.
- Own a machine that allows you to record your favorite TV shows so you can watch them whenever it's convenient for you—and you can even fast-forward through the commercials.
- Turn on your computer and be able to see on the screen the people you're talking to. There's no longer a need to travel for meetings.

Your reaction most likely would have been, "Wow! What am I going to do with all of my free time?" Maybe you would have started dreaming about a four-hour workweek. You'd be planning for all those extra tee times on the golf course. You'd be dreaming about spending time with your family or simply lying on a hammock in your backyard.

The fact is that's what technology *could have* enabled us to do. But instead of having more free time, we've added more things into our already crammed lives. Even though we get more and more done, we still pile up the tasks. Our calendars continuously stay full, no matter how many time-saving devices are invented.

As a result, we live our lives at warp speed. We've become champion multitaskers. We put our heads down and zip to work, dropping kids at school or daycare on the way. We eat on the run while having meetings on the fly. We get home late at night, watch TV, check our messages, hang out with our kids, send text messages, do the housework, pay the bills, and crash. Then we wake up the next day and do it all over again.

It's a dangerous way to live. And we, as pastors, confess that we're not immune. Both of us continually battle the temptation to live at an unhealthy pace. It's easy to justify this type of imbalance.

To help you identify imbalance in your life, you need to be aware of what we believe are three harmful lies at work in the lives of hurried and harried people, people just like us. These lies are insidious. They seem so harmless, but if we leave them unchecked and let them whisper to our minds, they can wreak havoc on our lives. Do you tell yourself any of these lies just to get through your day?

Lie #1: Things will settle down someday. The truth is that things will only settle down when you die or when you get intentional about adjusting your schedule. We tell ourselves things like, *If I can just get through next Wednesday, then everything's going to be fine.* But Wednesday comes, and things aren't fine. There's a new pressing deadline after that. And another after that.

Lie #2: More will be enough. With this lie we convince ourselves that we're just one more purchase or achievement away from contentment. If we could just *buy* more, *do* more, or *be* more, then things would be all right. But of course contentment never comes. As soon as we purchase, achieve, or obtain whatever it is we want, there's always something shinier, newer, and more alluring right around the next corner.

Lie #3: Everybody lives like this. This lie makes us believe that being overly busy is simply a way of life in our culture. Everybody lives at a frantic pace, so we need to follow suit. The truth is everyone doesn't live like this. Believe it or not, there are actually healthy people out there.[1]

The healthiest person who ever lived was Jesus. He got a lot done, but when we read about his life, the word *hurried* never comes to mind. Jesus came to offer us a different way of living. He said, "I have come that they may have life and have it to the full" (John 10:10). He wasn't talking about "full" in the sense of having a packed schedule. He meant it in the sense of abundance. In other words, a good, meaningful life.

Difficult Decisions

I (Dave) recently learned this lesson through one of my greatest passions—sports. Along with the day-to-day activities that include family, work, eating, and sleeping, I dedicate a good chunk of my time to my love of sports. It's easy for me to eat, sleep, and breathe basketball, baseball, football, golf, and pretty much anything else that happens to be on ESPN. Baseball is my favorite. I loved playing baseball when I was younger and I love watching baseball today. And just recently, I have fallen back in love with coaching baseball.

Fortunately for me, my wife, Lauren, is also a huge sports fan. She was and is a great athlete, and both of us grew up in worlds where we understood the amount of determination, passion, and effort it takes to succeed at sports. As you might have guessed, our love of sports has filtered down throughout our entire family.

Lauren and I have four kids, the oldest of whom is our nine-year-old son, Ethan, who also loves baseball. Actually I am not sure if he loves baseball or if I have just imposed my will on him. But for now, let's just assume that he really does love the game. Ethan has good hand-eye coordination, and it appears that he has the potential to be a pretty decent athlete.

But here's where things get a little sticky. As a coach, I know that intrinsic athletic ability is important. As a former high school baseball coach, I know you have to have some God-given talent to be able to catch, throw, hit, and be a solid baseball player. But I also know that what separates the decent athletes from the really good athletes is repetition. That means practices and games—and lots and lots and lots of them.[2] Athletic ability is *really* important, but repetition is *really, really, really* important.

The single best way to become good at anything is to do it over and over again. So if you want to give your child the best chance at succeeding in any sport, you have to start him or her early. You need to get your kids into the best leagues, the ones that practice and play a lot, and you have to make sacrifices. To nurture a kid into becoming a truly great athlete, it takes money, effort, sweat, and more money. And, by far, the single biggest sacrifice that families need to make for their kids to succeed in sports is time.

Where we live, there is a high-level baseball program that requires kids to practice three times a week and play forty-plus games a year. Yep, forty games, even for nine-year-old children. And for better or worse, Ethan is extremely competitive; if given the option, he would surely choose to play as much as humanly possible. But Lauren and I knew that if we went that route, our schedules would have to revolve around baseball for six months a year, leaving little time for much else, particularly for being present in our own lives and neighborhood.

The good news is that there is also a youth recreational league nearby. Anyone can sign up, and they assign teams based simply on geography. In this league, they play only eight games per season.

As Lauren and I became convicted about being better neighbors, it was clear which league Ethan would join, even if it meant that it would impact his development as a baseball player. This decision was not easy, but it became clear that it was necessary if we were to take the Great Commandment literally.

Sure, we've wrestled with our decision. The voices, both external and internal, tell us that we might be preventing Ethan from reaching his true potential. Absolutely, we love our son and want him to have the best opportunities available. And placing our son in the eight-game-per-season baseball league may mean we are putting him on a track that will hinder him from becoming as good an athlete as he probably could have been had we pushed him harder. And, sure, that wasn't an easy decision for two overly competitive, sports-loving parents. But we made the decision and, surprisingly, we are at peace with it.

Basically the decision boiled down to the need for us to figure out what was more important and then actually to live by that decision. Was our son's possible athletic career most important? Or was it more important for our family to live a nonfrenzied pace of life?

Choices

Our path may not be the route that God is asking you to take. Everyone is busy, and we all have different stories and struggle with different issues that compete for our attention and our time. We all should be concerned about how much we cram into our schedules. If we truly want to be great neighbors, we are going to have to make some adjustments. And that may mean God will call you to say no to some good things so you can focus on the things that are really important.

Certainly Jesus modeled this lifestyle. Many times he stopped his planned agenda to turn aside and care for someone else who seemed to be interrupting him. For instance, as

Jesus was walking along one day, a blind man yelled at Jesus to have mercy on him. The disciples considered the blind man a distraction. But Jesus stopped, talked to the man, and healed him.

Another time Jesus welcomed little children onto his lap, even though the disciples thought the kids were keeping him from more pressing matters. In yet another instance, Jesus was called on to heal an important official's daughter. As he headed down the road to the official's house, a woman with a health problem got his attention, and he stopped and healed her.

So let's think about this. Jesus got a lot done but he never seemed to be in a hurry. He lived a passionate, purposeful life but was never in a rush. The question for us, then, is how can we live like Jesus? The answer: we must learn how to keep the main thing the main thing.

Being Intentional

A friend of ours, Brian Mavis, recently said something to us that resonated.

"In this life, we can do only a few things really well; I think it's a good idea to make certain that one of those things is what Jesus says is most important."

His attitude echoes what we believe is an important first step to good neighboring—taking stock of our priorities and analyzing how we spend our time. As Psalm 90:12 says, "Teach us to number our days aright, that we may gain a heart of wisdom."

The psalmist is saying that if we can grasp our limitations, we may choose to prioritize differently. No question, we all have limited time and energy. And if we don't purposefully choose how we will spend it, those choices will be made for us. In essence, we just let life happen, passively. Time spent surfing the internet, playing video games, or just watching reruns of our favorite sitcoms won't amount to anything of value.

Of course we're not suggesting you eliminate such downtime activities from your schedule, because relaxation is beneficial. But it's also these mundane activities that can swallow up the margin of our lives if we aren't intentional. We are merely suggesting that you make room for other, more meaningful endeavors.

The Good, for the Great

In Luke 10 there's a story that points to a better way. Right after the story of the good Samaritan is one about Mary and Martha, two sisters who invite Jesus and some of his disciples into their home for a meal.

While Mary sits at the feet of Jesus listening to all he says, the other sister, Martha, devotes herself to cleaning the house and making the meal. The pace catches up with Martha, and she complains to Jesus. She wonders why her sister doesn't help her in the kitchen, according to the cultural practice of the day.

"'Martha, Martha,' the Lord answered, 'you are worried and upset about many things, but only one thing is needed. Mary has chosen what is better, and it will not be taken away from her'" (vv. 41–42).

There's a lot we can learn from Martha. The key phrase in this lesson is found in verse 40: "Martha was distracted by all the preparations that had to be made." At first glance, it looks like Martha is the one who really understands what's important in life. Martha opens up her home for Jesus. She cares so much about him and his followers that she prepares a meal. That's all good. But Martha's busyness causes her to miss out on an opportunity to be with Jesus and the others. And Jesus reprimands her for it.

This is crazy. Martha gets reprimanded *for serving Jesus.* But that's exactly what makes this story so powerful. Jesus is saying that sometimes we have to learn how to say no to good things to focus on what's most important.

Take another look at Mary. In particular, this one sentence is significant: Mary "sat at the Lord's feet listening to what he said." In Hebrew culture, to sit at someone's feet indicates a relationship between a disciple and a teacher. In that culture, however, women weren't supposed to be students, much less disciples of a rabbi. They were supposed to be in the kitchen helping fix a meal; a woman's identity was intertwined with her ability to be a good hostess. But Mary defies the cultural norms of her day. Instead, her life is centered around the main thing.

Similarly, if we're going to love our neighbors well, we, like Mary, must go against the grain. We must make time to listen carefully to the teachings of Jesus in the Great Commandment. Our purpose in life is to love God and love others. That may mean that sometimes we need to forego some good things to devote time and energy to better things, the main things—loving God and loving our neighbors. Living a hurried, frantic lifestyle is the opposite of what Jesus wants for our lives. Author John Ortberg has coined the phrase "hurry sickness." As he says, "Love and hurry are fundamentally incompatible. Love always takes time, and time is the one thing hurried people don't have."[3]

Ortberg is correct to identify hurriedness as a toxin. For example, can you remember a time when you were with someone and sensed he or she was trying to rush you? Or can you remember a time when you were trying to rush someone else? Did you feel loved in this exchange? And for that matter, did the other person?

More Time Today

If relationships are a priority, then what are some ways we can truly devote time to them? Perhaps much of your time is focused on building relationships with others based primarily on convenience: soccer parents, co-workers, or a small group of longtime friends. And there's nothing wrong with that. Quite frankly, if you're working at all on building connections with others, working on these relationships is a step in the right direction.

But we must also keep learning what it means to interpret the Great Commandment literally. In other words, we have to stop making it about what's only convenient to us and our often self-serving interpretation of the commandment. Instead we must start seeing our literal neighbors for who they are—our neighbors.

Yes, sometimes the term *neighbor* is used in its broadest sense. We're called to love all people, everywhere. But it's easy to use this metaphorical definition of neighbor—the world—as our only definition. And if that definition is our default, it probably means that by trying to love many, we actually love very few. Therefore, we should start with our most obvious neighbors—the ones that live nearest to us.

So if our lives are out of balance and we don't have time to get to know the person next door, the solution is clear— identify and eliminate the nonessentials. Following are three life-balancing principles that will help you do just that: (1) make the main thing the main thing, (2) eliminate time stealers, and (3) be interruptible.

Make the Main Thing the Main Thing

Making the main thing the main thing means taking time to reflect on what is most important in your life and then scheduling around those things. Be intentional about planning your life around the priorities you identify. This might mean planning time to just hang out on your block.

To understand this point, imagine three buckets that are almost full: a bucket of sand, a bucket of water, and a bucket of baseball-size rocks. The challenge is to put the contents of all of the buckets into one. The secret is starting with the rocks, then pouring in the sand so it fills the spaces around the rocks. The final step is pouring the water in so it filters through the sand and fills the bucket.

The lesson is that all the important things fit, as long as you start with the big items first. For us it means prioritizing our life with God first, followed by our life with our family. Then we suggest you prioritize the thing that Jesus says is most important—your neighbors. If you mix up the order, though, you won't be able to make it all fit. And if you don't set your priorities, others will do it for you.

Eliminate Time Stealers

Don't be afraid to say no to time stealers that get in the way of your top priorities. Not many people would say that watching TV, surfing the web, or playing video games truly enhances their life. These pastimes aren't evil, just useless. We have to learn how to stop wasting time with the activities that contribute nothing positive to our life. To do so, you have to learn the art of elimination; sometimes saying no is the best thing you can do.

If you ever find yourself in Florence, Italy, you should go see *David*, the statue by Michelangelo. If you do, you'll likely hear the guide tell the in-depth story of how Michelangelo carved the masterpiece. By Michelangelo's own account, he simply started with a block of marble and took away everything that wasn't the masterpiece. He was a master of the art of elimination. In the same way, when we take the Great Commandment seriously, we, too, must practice the art of elimination. We must focus on our top priorities and choose not to do the activities that keep us from that focus.

Be Interruptible

The idea of being interruptible is being willing to be inconvenienced. It means developing a mind-set that accepts the interruptions of others. This might not feel natural at first, but it's part of living at a healthy pace. I (Jay) have learned this the hard way. I grew up as an only child, so being flexible doesn't come as naturally to me as it might for others. But I have discovered the value of putting my agenda to the side and allowing others to enter my daily life.

My natural instinct is to do what I want, when I want to, and how I want to. But I have learned how to create some space in my life to be able to notice others when they are in need. Some simple shifts have made a big difference. But, if I'm not careful, I will fill up my weekends. We all have a lot of errands to run and to-do boxes to check off. This eventually makes us hurried on the inside and out. When we create the right kind of margins, however, we can live with a level of peace that allows us to be interruptible.

An Art Not a Science

Last Halloween, I (Dave) discovered just how difficult the art of neighboring can be when it comes to scheduling. Our family was invited to two events: a neighborhood party and a get-together for all my old college buddies and their families. The events were on the same night, and I wrestled with what to do.

I could make a great case in my own mind for seeing all my old college buddies again. I don't get to see them as often as I used to and I always have a great time when we are together. And unlike some of our neighbors, I have a lot in common with my college buddies. I actually chose them, whereas I didn't choose my neighbors.

Still, my wife and I have made it a priority in our lives to be committed to spending time with our neighbors.

So what did we do? We went to the neighborhood party, left after a couple of hours, and then went over to the party with my college buddies. We stayed a while and ended up driving back to our neighbors' party. That night we chose both.

In essence, I "interrupted" my original plan to accommodate a new one, thus inviting the opportunity to forge neighborhood friendships, while still maintaining old friendships.

Did we make the right choice? Debatable. Perhaps we tried to do too much and ended up just skimming the surface at both places. Being a good neighbor is an art not a science. But I think if we were to do it again, we'd probably say no to the party with my friends from college. There are only so many people you can go deep with.

So keep in mind that if you take the journey toward neighboring, you'll be faced with tough decisions like these. Sure, going to my friends' party might have been a *good* choice, but going to the neighbors' party might have been the *better* choice. That's part of what we're still learning.

Important questions to ask yourself, then, are, *Do I live at a pace that allows me to be available to those around me? And if not, are all of the things I'm doing more important than taking the Great Commandment literally?*

We know that we need to reprioritize our lives. And the bottom line is that it will take some real courage to begin to eliminate and create enough space to be great neighbors. Remember, real relationships with our neighbors will happen as we have the ability to be present and connected to them. It's one thing to be home; it's another thing to be present. It's going to take some real discipline with our calendars and our hearts to become the kind of neighbors that Jesus wants us to be. But it's worth it.

4

The Fear Factor

When my family and I (Jay) moved into our neighborhood, one of the first things Danielle did was bake apple pies. She loves baking, so sharing her treats was an easy way to introduce ourselves to our new neighbors. We didn't want to wait for them to make the first move, which we thought could be awkward.

Then we learned how truly awkward this process can be. The good news is that we encountered mostly positive responses. People were appreciative and thanked us for the pies. Others were surprised, almost a bit embarrassed, that they hadn't done something to welcome us first. But most seemed happy to see us, and we enjoyed meeting them.

One of our neighbors, however, went in the complete opposite direction. He wouldn't even open the door to say hello. And when Danielle and I approached, he spoke to us only from a tiny crack in the door. He actually told us to leave! It was as though he thought we were there to sell something or distribute religious literature.

"We just want to give you a pie," we said. "We just moved in around the corner, and we're taking pies to all our neighbors."

"Whatever you're selling, we don't want it," he said. "If it's a sample, you can leave it on the doorstep."

"We're not selling anything," we said, pointing to our home, two hundred feet away. "We live right over there."

"No, we don't need anything. Just go away!"

So we did.

On the way back home, Danielle and I discussed what had just happened. I mean, seriously, what could be threatening about apple pie?

We tried to put ourselves in our neighbor's shoes. It sounded as if he spoke with an accent, so maybe our American forwardness was too over the top for his cultural upbringing. Or perhaps no one had ever reached out and tried to get to know him. This neighbor had also asked us several times if we were solicitors. Did he just not believe us when we said no? Regardless, we couldn't help but take it personally. The episode left us feeling very confused.

A few days later, I spotted this same neighbor out in front of his home doing yard work. I walked over and introduced myself again. This time he was a bit more receptive. He told me that the only people who ever came to the door were salespeople, and he thought for sure we were selling something. I reassured him (again) that we were not. Even after that positive exchange, it still took the family a while to warm up to us. If we saw them driving in the neighborhood, we waved, but they didn't wave back. Eventually, though, they returned our wave.

So what was up with our neighbor? As we got to know him better, we realized that he was really just afraid—afraid of the unknown. He had fallen prey to one of the primary obstacles to neighboring in our culture today: fear.

Nonstop News

It's no wonder we live in a culture of fear and suspicion, given the twenty-four-hour news cycle that's just one click away. Anytime, any day, you can turn on the TV or hit a link to view multiple scary or downright cringe-worthy stories. The natural response is, "Wow, we live in a sick and broken world." And it's true—there are some really messed up people out there.

The problem is that when we are continually exposed to these types of stories, a subtle shift can take place in how we view the people around us. It's easy to believe that those really sick people are everywhere, when, in reality, they are the exception. And you can't help but wonder, are there just that many more sick people in the world than in generations past? Or is it possible that, because of technology, our awareness of people's brokenness is much higher now than it has been in the past?

These days it's easy to be suspicious of people you don't know:

- Perhaps there's a man who lives alone on your block. And for some reason, you've always had an uncomfortable feeling whenever you see him.

- Maybe there are kids in your neighborhood who are about the same age as yours. But you know that their parents don't have the same values as you do, and you feel a bit uneasy every time your kids ask to go over there and play.

- How about that house on your block where nobody ever seems to be home? It's not abandoned; it's just that no one is ever there. You wonder what in the world is wrong with those people.

- Is there a family on your block that always seems to have drama in their lives? You can tell that they have a ton of baggage, and maybe you're just not sure if you want to enter into their chaos. It's just easier to keep them at a healthy distance.

- Or maybe it's the idea of long-term commitment. You know that if you get to know a particular neighbor, you're going to be in one another's lives for years to come. Going down to the soup kitchen one night a year is one thing, but when you get to know your neighbors, they're *always* there. There's no getting away from them, nowhere to run and hide.

We're not recommending that you simply dismiss all of your fears and blindly jump into every one of your neighbors' lives. After all, at times our fears are valid and can save us from dangerous and unhealthy situations. On the other hand, our fears are often unwarranted and may be obstacles to obeying the Great Commandment. So if we're going to neighbor well, we must have the courage to wrestle with our fears.

A few years ago Lauren and I (Dave) went to a party at one of our neighbor's homes shortly after moving into our first neighborhood. To put it nicely, there was a lot of drinking going on. Now, if you are going to learn how to neighbor well, then you are going to need to get comfortable in environments where alcohol is being consumed. There's a difference, however, between people having a few beers and being hammered by 4:00 p.m. on a Saturday afternoon.

At this particular party, a number of people were getting sloppy drunk before sundown. Our kids were very young back then, and both Lauren and I felt unnerved about exposing them to adults who were clearly very intoxicated. Worse yet, we weren't the only ones who brought our kids; there were kids running around everywhere. And we started to wonder if this should have been an adults-only party.

A series of questions began to run through our minds. Should we make up an excuse to leave? To be honest, that didn't seem like the right thing to do. Should we hold on to our kids or tell them that they had to be next to us at all times? Anyone with children knows that's a ridiculous notion. Or should we let our kids become friends with their kids?

I remember after that party, Lauren and I really struggled to figure out what we should do when faced with such dilemmas in the future. Looking back, the main thing it forced us to do was to ask God to lead us as we engaged our neighborhood. We believe this is what God wants of each of us. After praying about it, we decided to continue attending the parties while keeping a very close eye on our kids.

To be sure, throughout this journey we have often thought, *This neighboring stuff is just too messy. I'm just not sure it's worth it.* And being honest here—you may get to a point where you too just want to throw in the towel. But fortunately we are learning the value of leaning in and embracing the tension. All you can do is remember the words of Jesus. Remember that neighboring really matters. And remember that being a good neighbor is something that both changes the people who live around us and changes us as well. As Lauren and I wrestled through the situation with the party, we found ourselves asking God for guidance. And as a result, we grew closer to him.

Grasshoppers and Giants

When the Israelites first considered entering the Promised Land, they came to the border and stopped. In Numbers 13 we read their story. The Israelites sent twelve spies into the land, and all except two came back with fearful reports. "The land is fantastic," said the ten fearful spies. "Everywhere we looked, the whole country flowed with milk and honey. But the people who live there are giants, and there is absolutely no way that we Israelites could ever take possession of the land." They even went so far as to say that their enemies saw them as nothing more than grasshoppers.

However, two of the spies, Joshua and Caleb, saw things differently. They could see that fear was distracting the others from the promise of God's provision. The fear was all in the ten spies' perception, declared Joshua and Caleb. Did the other spies ever actually interview the people to find out how scary they really were? Though there was much to be afraid of (fortified walls, potential for war, better weapons), there was no way that they could tell what their enemies were thinking. They weren't mind readers. Did their enemies really see the Israelites as mere grasshoppers, or was that only how the ten fearful spies perceived the situation? What we're saying is that fear changes not only our image of others but also what we assume they think about us.

Unfortunately the nation of Israel believed the ten fearful spies. So God became angry at their cowardice and lack of faith, and as a result, they spent forty years wandering in the wilderness. They were on the doorstep of something that God wanted to do through them, but their perceived fears kept them from what God had laid out for them.

Forty years later the Israelites came to the border of the Promised Land again. Everyone from the previous generation, except Joshua and Caleb, had died. A telling statement comes from Rahab, a woman who lived in the land. She explained how, years earlier, things were the opposite of what the Israelites thought was true. Joshua and Caleb had been right all along. When the spies entered the land forty years earlier, everybody in the land was afraid of them. They did not see them as easy prey, as the ten spies had imagined.

> [Rahab] said to them, "I know that the LORD has given you this land and that a great fear of you has fallen on us, so that all who live in this country are melting in fear because of you. We have heard how the LORD dried up the water of the Red Sea for you when you came out of Egypt, and what you did to Sihon and Og, the two kings of the Amorites east of the Jordan, whom you completely destroyed. When we heard of

it, our hearts melted in fear and everyone's courage failed because of you, for the LORD your God is God in heaven above and on the earth below." (Josh. 2:9–11)

The Israelites' perception had been wrong all along. They had always feared their neighbors, perceiving them as giants. But in truth their neighbors feared the Israelites because of their God.

Fear has a way of distorting our perspective. When we are afraid of others, we think of ourselves as less important and less powerful. The world is big, bad, and dark, but Rahab's words can give us encouragement when applied to our situation. We may be afraid, but often things are not as they seem. When we are following God into our neighborhoods, we have nothing to fear. And often it's our neighbors that need to be rescued from their fear.

And keep in mind that most of us have been conditioned to be afraid of our neighbors, and they've been conditioned to be afraid of us. Someone has to break the cycle of fear. God has given us an invitation to go forward not backward. First Peter 3:13–16 offers a further perspective. Peter asks:

> Who is going to harm you if you are eager to do good? But even if you should suffer for what is right, you are blessed. "Do not fear their threats; do not be frightened." But in your hearts revere Christ as Lord. Always be prepared to give an answer to everyone who asks you to give the reason for the hope that you have. But do this with gentleness and respect, keeping a clear conscience.

This text is often applied in the context of apologetics and learning how to explain to people what we believe: that we should always be prepared to give an answer to anyone who asks about our hope in Jesus. Yet notice the surrounding context. Peter is quoting from Isaiah 8:12, and the instruction is clear. When you encounter other people, *do not fear. Do not be frightened.* Even when everyone around you chooses fear, you have a hope that is greater. Live out that hope, and don't be afraid to talk about it.

Balancing our fears and discernment is another issue that we all must confront. When it comes to meeting your neighbors for the first time, you don't want to abandon your discernment. And certainly caution is justified when you encounter strangers.

Yet there is often a part of fear that isn't justified, and you have to push past it. Be thoughtful about whom you approach and how. But also know, at the end of the day, following Jesus is not necessarily designed to be safe. Safety is a natural desire but it can keep us from being like Jesus in the midst of an unsafe world. Actually, much of our "fear" is better labeled "timidity." It can happen when there is an awkward lapse in social interaction, when a pause lasts too long. Or perhaps someone tells a joke and no one laughs. Or maybe you don't know what to say first. It can be hard to break the ice. Sure, it doesn't feel natural to walk up to a stranger's door and offer her a pie you've just baked. These are the times when you whisper to yourself things like: "This is strange. These people are going to think that this is really weird." Or "I'm an introvert and there has to be someone on this block better suited for this." Even "This isn't the right time; maybe I'll take the initiative and meet them next week" (or next month, or next year). This feeling of awkwardness isn't fear—it's just nervousness about possible rejection. The truth is, awkwardness won't kill you.

In 2 Timothy Paul writes: "For the Spirit God gave us does not make us timid, but gives us power, love and self-discipline" (1:7). God enables all of us to be bold, to take the first step, to be the neighbor we were meant to be. We don't need to be afraid. When we feel those emotions creeping in, we need to remind ourselves that enduring awkwardness is probably the worst of it.

Moving to the Front Yard

Tom and Angela had lived in their neighborhood for about twelve years without really getting to know many people. They lived in a cul-de-sac of eleven houses and had limited communication and interaction with the people around them. They admitted that this felt strange because they really had a desire to know their neighbors better, but nobody was making the first move. With the exception of a smile and wave as they passed their neighbors in their cars, nothing really happened. A number of years went by until finally Tom and Angela decided to do something.

One of the biggest factors that had been preventing them from engaging their neighbors was timidity. They were apprehensive about taking the first step, about being socially uncomfortable, particularly when so much time had already passed.

They began by taking one simple step. They switched yards. Their kids had always played in the backyard, and that setting was the social hub of the family. So Tom and Angela simply switched to the front yard. They put up a swing in a front-yard tree and added some lawn chairs; that was about it.

Nothing happened at first. Then over the next few weeks, children and even dogs began to migrate into their front yard. Eventually adults followed. Soon both kids and adults were spending more time in their front yard than they could ever have imagined. And all they had done to attract this traffic was hang out where they could be seen.

Then Tom and Angela decided to go a step further by organizing a series of block parties. Surprisingly, the first one they held went over quite well. All the neighbors really needed was someone to step forward and break the ice.

Other parties followed. Sometimes it was a barbecue in someone's backyard. Other times they organized potlucks at someone's house. And a few times they went all out and rented one of those bouncy houses for kids—a really big draw!

The results were powerful. Barriers were broken down, and people started getting to know each other. Soon they were inviting one another into their homes. Neighbors began to assist neighbors in various ways. For a time, Tom and Angela were able to look after a neighborhood girl after school until her mom came home from work.

"Over the last two years, we've really gotten to know each other better as neighbors," Tom says. "A year ago, one of the couples on our block went through a divorce. Because of our preexisting relationship, the husband approached me, and we spent almost three hours in our driveway talking about what was going on. This type of interaction just would not have been possible without all of the prior time together. Not only would he not have been willing to share, but I don't think I would have been likely to give him the attention he needed.

"Many of our neighbors still tend to 'hibernate' during the winter months. But by spending time together each summer, we've developed a level of trust and respect for each other."

God is already working in your neighborhood. Being a good neighbor simply means slowing down and being aware of what he is designing. By developing real relationships, you'll find out how God is already moving in a person's life. You'll begin to overcome the fear that you once had and develop trust for one another.

Fear and Isolation

A friend of ours, Wes, runs a homeless shelter. A while back he mentioned to us that most of the people in his shelter ended up there because of isolation. They became distanced from friends, family, and neighbors. And then it took only one bad break for them to end up on the streets.

The genius of good neighboring is that it combats such isolation. Taking that pie across the street or just walking over and learning someone's name addresses the issue of isolation in our neighborhoods.

Remember, it's easy to make assumptions about other people when you don't really know anything about them. So just continually examine the assumptions or perceptions that you have about your neighbors. Ask yourself, *Is this an assumption or is this true? Maybe if I got to know him, I would feel different.*

Confronting our fears regarding our neighbors can be hard work, but it is worth it. There's a lot of peace that can come to your life when you know your neighbors. You can grow to be a person who isn't controlled by fear, a much better way to live.

5

Moving Down the Line

ecently I (Dave) was in my living room working on my laptop when I happened to glance out the window and see my neighbor Eric. He was working on a car I didn't recognize. I don't know much about cars. Actually I know next to nothing about cars. However, I was curious and knew that this was an opportunity both to procrastinate and to interact with my neighbor. So I simply walked outside and asked Eric what he was up to and if there was anything that I could do to help.

All I did that afternoon was close up my laptop and walk outside. Yet that ended up leading me into a great conversation. Eric and I talked for twenty minutes, and he told me that the car was actually his son's and not his. His son had recently bought the car, and it was already having some issues.

Pretty soon the conversation had moved to something more significant than cars.

Eric shared that his son had a lot going on, and he was worried about him and some of his recent decisions. A simple conversation about a broken car ended up becoming a conversation of depth. We both left knowing each other a little better. It all started when I glanced out my window and made a decision to walk outside and say hello.

Have you ever stared into your garage and thought, *I know that I need to spend a day cleaning this place but I just don't know where to begin*? Neighboring can be like that for many of us. Knowing where to start is sometimes the hardest step. In moving from theory to practice, we can sometimes become immobilized while trying to figure out what do to.

Believe me, I understand it can feel foreign and very uncomfortable to undertake something new. When Facebook first started gaining traction, I decided it was going to be a fad. I wasn't going to waste my time adding another thing to my life that I needed to manage. Also it seemed weird to me to take time to tell everyone where I was and what I had for breakfast.

But after a year or so of being stubborn, I finally broke down and joined the rest of the world on Facebook. For the first couple of weeks, I wasn't a big fan. I couldn't fully grasp how everything worked, and, to be honest, it was kind of uncomfortable knowing that a bunch of people I haven't talked to in years would be reading what I was posting. Needless to say, after taking some time to play around with it and learning the different nuances, I became a fully functioning Facebook user. I was even enjoying it. Something that felt foreign to me at first became very comfortable and enjoyable once I made a decision to give just a little effort.

The same is true when it comes to the art of neighboring. In the beginning it can sometimes feel awkward or strange. After all, we are talking about interacting with strangers. But if you are willing to lean into the process and make an effort, you will be surprised at the results. We developed a simple framework that has proven to be a helpful tool for people who are trying to figure out where to start and then how to continue being a better neighbor:

Stranger → Acquaintance → Relationship

From Stranger to Acquaintance

When you did the block map exercise in chapter 2, you identified the people in the eight houses closest to you whom you know by name. The people you don't know by name are strangers. You might occasionally see them, and they have hopefully seen you, but the level of your interaction with them is minimal; perhaps it's been only a wave from the car on the way to work in the morning. You may even know something about them, but the bottom line is if you don't know their name, you really don't know them.

The first step to taking the Great Commandment literally is to move from stranger to acquaintance in your relationships with those who live nearest to you. Learning a person's name is the first and easiest step you can take to become a better neighbor. Have you been able to fill in any more of the blank spaces on your block map since you first completed the exercise? If so, keep up the good work. If not, you should stop reading this book and go take a walk around your block.

Trust me (Dave), learning names is not one of my strengths. I am not known for being able to pay attention for long periods of time. And by that I mean anything over thirty seconds. No one has ever accused me of being an incredible listener, and if Ritalin had been prevalent when I was in school, I am sure I would have been on the highest dosage.

So when I finished the block map exercise for the first time and began to think about introducing myself to the neighbors I didn't know by name, I had a sickening realization. While I didn't know some of my neighbors' names, I had actually met most of them before—in some cases multiple times. The problem was that I had not made it a priority to remember their names. As I began to think of ways to avoid having to admit this to their face, I felt convicted and decided to use this as motivation to interact with them again.

Over the span of a week or so, I made it a point to talk with my neighbors whom I didn't know by name. The conversation usually started with my walking over to them as they were coming or going and saying, "Hey, I'm Dave. I know that you have told me your name before, but I'm not great with names and have forgotten it." On more than one occasion, I can also remember saying, "Hey, we wave to each other all the time, but I actually don't know your name."

Then my wife and I started to do something *very* important. We wrote down the names we were learning on a simple block map that we taped to the side of the fridge. This may not seem like a big deal, but it was. Once we put the chart up where we could see it every day, we found ourselves thinking more and more about the neighbors that we knew by name *and* about the ones we needed to introduce ourselves to when the opportunity arose.

The block map, as we now refer to it, is a tool that we believe in because it helps us remember names. It is also a tangible way for us to know if we are, at the very least, acquaintances with the people God has placed around us.

As we began to realize the power of learning names, Lauren took the idea one step further and created a block directory. One of the homes on our block was recently burglarized, and Lauren used that as an opportunity to go door-to-door and gather contact information. She thought it was a good idea to create a basic information sheet that would enable us to better communicate with one another. Almost everyone agreed. So Lauren put together a simple map of the neighborhood, including everybody's name, home and cell numbers, and email addresses. Then she gave a copy to everyone on the block.

It's hard to explain just how valuable this fairly simple tool has become in our neighborhood. For starters, it gave everyone in our neighborhood a way to look up the names of everyone else. It also made it easy for us to communicate with one another. Since creating the block directory, there have been numerous times that we have received calls from neighbors because, for example, our garage door was left open late at night or they needed to borrow something.

What's more, awhile back, one of the women in the neighborhood used the email addresses to invite all of the other women for a girls' night out. The contact information in our block directory became significant because it helped facilitate and further new relationships. Just from creating this simple tool, not only have we been able to move to the acquaintance stage with all of our neighbors, but many of our neighbors have also been able to do the same.

From Acquaintance to Relationship

Once you have learned and remembered someone's name, your relationship has moved from stranger to acquaintance. That's a crucial first step. However, Jesus didn't tell us to become acquaintances with our neighbors; he called us to love them, and that means we need to have an actual relationship with them.

But moving from acquaintance to relationship is not as clean or as easily defined as the first step. There isn't a simple tool that can move you into relationship, because it is impossible to program relationships. All of us can, however, create environments where relationships might develop and grow into something significant.

Vicky Reier, assistant city manager in Arvada, Colorado, has taught our network of churches a lot when it comes to neighboring. At one of our pastors' gatherings, Vicky challenged us to encourage and equip the people in our churches to throw block parties. She said that it may not sound like a big deal, but a block party movement could have an incredible, long-term impact in our community. We have taken Vicky's words to heart and have been amazed to see how effective parties can be in fostering neighbor relations. Now, we are not talking about an annual HOA (homeowners association) block party that only 10 percent of the subdivision attends. When we use the term *block party*, we are talking about a party that is thrown by and attended by people who live on a specific block or group of blocks.

Block parties are natural environments in which neighbors will often take steps from being acquaintances to actually being friends. Parties create space for us to talk to others we already know and to meet people we don't. Maybe this is the reason Jesus spent so much time at parties—he knew the power of a party. He understood they were an important means for people to share their lives with one another in very real and practical ways.

In the book of Luke we read the account of Jesus calling Levi to be one of his disciples and then Levi responding by throwing a party. The story is in 5:27–32.

> After this, Jesus went out and saw a tax collector by the name of Levi sitting at his tax booth. "Follow me," Jesus said to him, and Levi got up, left everything and followed him.
>
> Then Levi held a great banquet for Jesus at his house, and a large crowd of tax collectors and others were eating with them. But the Pharisees and the teachers of the law who belonged to their sect complained to his disciples, "Why do you eat and drink with tax collectors and sinners?"
>
> Jesus answered them, "It is not the healthy who need a doctor, but the sick. I have not come to call the righteous, but sinners to repentance."

There's a lot that happens in this short account. When Levi throws this party, Jesus is more than happy to attend. After all, Levi is creating an environment where the people he knows well can interact with Jesus and his new friends. From all indications, Jesus doesn't even think twice about showing up to this event, although he knows it's likely he is going to be criticized by some of the religious leaders for attending.

Let's be honest. The fact that the Pharisees question Jesus's attendance indicates that this party was likely not a "Mountain Dew and pizza" kind of party. This, for sure, wasn't a Sunday afternoon church potluck. This was a party where people were having a lot of fun.

So when the Pharisees question him, Jesus has every opportunity to apologize for spending time with "sinners." Yet Jesus actually does the opposite. He defends his right to be there and doesn't back down because he is using the opportunity to hang out and party with a group of people who don't have any religious framework and whom he might not see otherwise.

When is the last time you were accused of doing something like this? Has your character ever been questioned because you ate or drank with sketchy people? Not everyone in the neighborhood is cleaned up and easy to be around. We need to be willing to follow Jesus and choose to be with others in uncomfortable situations, because we can't always expect people to come onto our turf; we must also be willing to enter their world.

Let's make this personal. When we participate in block parties, we are being like Jesus. We are making it a priority to understand the people God has placed around us, regardless of what they believe or how they act.

You may wonder, *Wouldn't it have made more sense for Jesus to throw the party to celebrate Levi's decision to follow him?* But that's not how the story goes. Levi is so excited about what is happening in his life that he gathers his circle of friends and invites Jesus and the disciples to join them in celebrating.

With this in mind, when we consider gathering our neighbors together, there may be others who are better suited to host the party. If so, look to partner with them rather than trying to plan and host a party on your own. If not, then maybe God wants you to be the one who initiates the gathering. Either way, as Christians, we should be playing a part in throwing the best parties in our neighborhoods—not sitting on the sidelines being irritated because the music is too loud.

There's Gold Next Door

Diane attends a church that a couple of years ago presented a sermon series on the art of neighboring. As she listened one Sunday morning, she found herself thinking about how different the neighborhood of her childhood was compared to the one she had been living in for more than a decade. She had always wished that she knew her neighbors better, and now she sensed that God was calling her to do something about it.

After hearing about the value of learning her neighbors' names, Diane went home and did something radical. She acted on what was discussed in church earlier that day. She decided to start taking walks and looking for opportunities to learn some of the names of the people she encountered.

While she was on one of her walks, she ran into an older lady that she had waved to numerous times in the past. This time Diane stopped and began talking to the woman. They both mentioned the fact that everyone in the neighborhood seems very busy these days. Then Diane's neighbor, a widow, mentioned that she had been having some health issues. When Diane showed concern, her neighbor shared with her that she had just finished treatments for cancer and that it looked like it was in remission. Diane is a cancer survivor as well, and immediately the two had a bond that most of us cannot understand.

Soon after that conversation, Diane ran into her new friend again. This time her neighbor began to share some of her story with Diane. She said she was born in Germany and had spent her childhood there. And then she shared that she was actually a Holocaust survivor. They talked for a while that day, and Diane walked back to her house with her mind spinning. It dawned on her that they had been living near each other for ten-plus years, and she was just now learning that her neighbor had an amazing life story.

When Diane shared this story with us, she made a statement that we have not forgotten. She said, "I am learning that there are people right around me that have incredible things to share with me and others. It's like I have been living next to a gold mine, but I was too busy to know there was gold right next door."

Diane's story didn't end there. As she began to fill in her block map, she felt an urge to gather her neighbors together. She printed up a simple flyer that outlined a plan for a block party the following month. Distributing the flyers personally gave Diane a chance to learn a bunch of new names, and she carried a small notepad to write them in as she went door-to-door. Diane's block map was quickly becoming a block directory.

Once they realized that her block party invite wasn't a flyer for a roofing company, most of the neighbors she met were very friendly. Many of them even expressed interest in contributing and helping out with the party.

A month later, Diane stood in front of her driveway and watched more than forty of her neighbors hang out together for the first time. For Diane the most rewarding part of the party occurred when a guy who had been known only as "the grumpy neighbor" came to the party. Not only was he not grumpy but he also brought over two canopies and set them up to provide shade for those who wanted it.

One of the longtime residents thanked Diane and mentioned that the neighborhood used to do this kind of stuff all the time. She said that, for some reason, the parties and gatherings stopped happening and this was the first block party anyone had organized in more than fifteen years.

Diane's story reminds us that there are amazing people and stories all around us. Often all we have to do is take a walk and be willing to engage the people we see along the way. By doing so, Diane moved from stranger to acquaintance with a number of her neighbors. And by initiating a block party, Diane helped to create an environment where many were able to get to know each other better. Diane and many others have embodied the neighboring framework that we believe works.

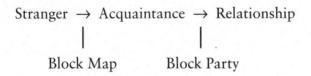

Stranger → Acquaintance → Relationship

Block Map   Block Party

It may sound weird to categorize levels of friendship, but we have found it's crucial to define where we really stand with our neighbors so we can know what to do next. And understanding the neighboring framework of stranger-acquaintance-relationship can help us accomplish just that. It prompts practical steps that we can take to make real progress.

So start asking yourself, *What would it be like if we were to make a commitment to take the next step with each of our immediate neighbors this year? What would it be like to make a commitment to throw at least one good block party every year, and then to sit back and see how God uses it on our block?*

For some of you, the idea of neighboring might seem overwhelming. Maybe you are an introvert. Maybe the idea of meeting new people is intimidating. Or maybe you have tried to be friendly and it just doesn't seem to be making a difference on your block. So we've made it easy for you: fill in the block map, plan a block party, and good things are sure to happen. Your first block party might not be all you are hoping for. You might only get one or two other families to come. That is still a huge success! Anytime we get two or more households to spend time together, it's a win. The key is to keep moving forward. Check out the website at www.artofneighboring.com for more resources to help you with your block party.

6

Baby Steps

nyone can be a good neighbor. And proof of that is an inspiring neighboring testimony we've heard from an eleven-year-old girl named Nicole.

A few years ago, Nicole's family made a commitment to reach out to their neighbors across the street. That family consisted of a recently divorced mom and seven foster kids. To say that their life was chaotic would be a massive under-statement. As they began to engage this family and learn about the complexity of their household, it began to feel overwhelming. Nicole noticed that two of their elementary-age kids were struggling. She mentioned to her mom that she would be willing to help them with their schoolwork a couple of times a week.

Nicole began tutoring these two kids. She knew she had something to offer, so she simply showed up at their house

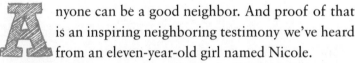

on Tuesdays and Thursdays to help. Not only is she serving these kids in significant ways, she is also serving their mom, who has expressed how grateful she is for the role Nicole is playing in the lives of her kids. This is a beautiful reminder of the power of neighboring. If an eleven-year-old child can figure out a way to match up her gifts with the needs of her neighbors, then so can you!

In our culture, we have a fascination with celebrities and talent. We are riveted by movies about extraordinary people doing extraordinary things because we want to be inspired and wowed by the lives of others.

So imagine watching a movie about a man who goes to work every day, has dinner with his family five nights a week, and reads books to his kids before they go to bed at night. He also is a great neighbor. He makes time to invite his neighbors over for a meal a few times a month. Instead of watching football games by himself, he watches them with the people who live around him. He lets his neighbors borrow his tools and helps them work on their cars. Occasionally he grabs a drink with a few of his neighbors and they talk about their jobs and what they think their kids will grow up to be. When one of his neighbors is going through a hard time, he's available. When a neighbor needs him to watch her kids because something unexpected comes up, he is always willing. Imagine in scene after scene of this film, we watch a man who is consistently faithful to love those who live nearest to him. This would be a terribly boring movie. No one would pay to see it.

The movies we watch tell us a lot about what we value in our culture. We don't value consistency. On the whole, we are convinced that we need to make a big splash to make a difference, that just being a good neighbor isn't that big a deal.

But Jesus says being a good neighbor is exactly the kind of life that can change the world. This simple truth can change everything: *small things matter*. They really do.

It doesn't take a superhero to be a great neighbor. We all wish we were a bit more of something—smarter, funnier, or wealthier. Often we have a hard time recognizing what we do have to offer. When it comes to neighboring, it's important to figure out how we can make a difference in the lives of our neighbors. It may not seem that we have much, but when we give from what we have, something sacred happens. God uses the small things that we bring to him and multiplies them into a miracle in someone else's life.

Give What You Have

There's a passage in Scripture about a small boy who becomes a hero. This boy is so insignificant that we don't even know his name, but he stands in a group of adults and gives what he has. Then a miracle takes place. His little effort combines with God's power, and everything changes. The story is found in all four Gospels, but John gives the most detailed account of this heroic boy's actions (6:1–13).

It's getting late, and thousands of people have hung around all day to listen to Jesus preach. But it's becoming clear that all of these people didn't plan ahead. They need to eat but they are miles from civilization. Jesus turns to his disciples and tells them to find something for the crowd for dinner.

But the disciples have no way of providing a meal for the crowd. One of the disciples, Philip, calculates what it would cost—more than a year's salary, way more than they can afford. Clearly the disciples are *way* over their heads with the challenge at hand. What is Jesus expecting? He's not serious, right?

When we start to take the Great Commandment literally, we realize we don't have what it takes. We don't have enough time, even though we prioritize. We aren't great at remembering names, even though we write them down and try to remember. We don't love enough, even though we are trying to be like Jesus. We feel as though we are being asked to manage an impossible task—loving our neighbors. Do our small efforts add up to anything? Let's get back to our story.

As the disciples are about to give up, something outlandish happens. "Another of his disciples, Andrew, Simon Peter's brother, spoke up, 'Here is a boy with five small barley loaves and two small fish, but how far will they go among so many?'" (vv. 8–9).

Andrew knows the little boy's lunch would feed only a few of the people. Why would he even offer something so ridiculous? First of all, it's rude. You shouldn't take food from little children. Second, it's silly. What good could it possibly accomplish? What was Andrew thinking? Apparently Andrew knew something we should all remember: small sacrifices can lead to a miracle. When you give what you have, even if it's minute, God can make a miracle. He can work with very little and turn it into something that no one could have imagined.

As the passage continues, Jesus prays for the food. Then he breaks up this kid's lunch and hands it out to the disciples. He tells them to start distributing it—somehow there is enough to feed the crowd.

Now here's an interesting question: When did the food multiply? As far as I (Jay) can tell, it could have happened one of two ways. Maybe after Jesus prayed, bucket loads of bread started falling from the sky. Whole fish dropped down in large piles, and the disciples started to grab handfuls and pass them out.

Fish and loaves didn't rain down from the sky. I think that the miracle happened in the hands of the disciples. As they handed out the bread and fish, it was miraculously replaced in their baskets. Every time they gave away some food, they looked down into the basket, only to find it full again. The miracle happened as they participated in giving the food away. The food multiplied in their hands.

Can you imagine being a part of something like this? It must have been amazing, not only for the disciples but for the little boy as well. Suddenly he is a hero. He gives up his lunch, and a bunch of adults get to participate in a miracle. I doubt he ever imagined his day would turn out like that.

When you give away what you have, Jesus will give you more to give. Even if what you have isn't enough to solve the whole problem, just do what you can in the moment—give it anyway. Trust that God will fill you up with enough to supply the need that's right in front of you, and assume he will do it again for the next need as well. If you don't give, you don't get a chance to see God do a miracle.

Just Do Something

We all assume someone else is the expert. But when it comes to loving our neighbors, every situation is different. Every neighbor is different, and every person who is trying to love others has a variety of gifts to offer. We all have various strengths and weaknesses. But if we allow ourselves to get involved in the lives of others, miracles can happen. God can intervene and do amazing things.

Many years ago our friend David took over a struggling church that had become fairly stagnant and uninspiring. Most of the people in the church weren't relating with anyone outside the church, and they didn't really have any kind of connection to their city. David knew that something had to be done; he just didn't know what. So he attended conferences at other successful churches. He started reading every popular book he could get his hands on about church growth and health. It was after learning about many different options that he began to ask God which one should be the path for his church. In prayer he started laying out all the possibilities, hoping God would lead him toward the best road. That's when he heard God say something to him, and it wasn't what he expected to hear. He heard clearly from God, Just do *something*.

The message for us? Just make some effort. And remember, relationships don't happen when we heap pressure onto ourselves and others. So don't try too hard! This can happen more easily than you anticipate because this is how God designed you to live. You were built to connect with other people. So be who you are, and relationships will grow out of that. It makes friendship normal and natural, something that just happens rather than something that's forced. And the most natural way to connect with people is through shared activities. Here are several examples of ways you can connect with those who live closest to you.

- *Baking/cooking.* We know lots of people who like to cook different types of tasty treats. And often those who love baking want an excuse to make a few pies or some brownies. Sharing some with the neighbors is a great way to connect with them. Sure, it's a bit of work. But if you're already inclined to do this, you'll enjoy the process.

- *Playing sports.* There are all kinds of ways that your neighbors are probably interacting with sports right now. Some are playing in leagues; some have kids who play. Some haven't been involved in sports lately because they have been too busy; they just need someone to give them an excuse to dust off those old golf clubs or put on those running shoes. All you need to do is ask them to come along with you.

- *Watching sports or other shows on TV.* There are probably neighbors around you who are watching the exact same sports event or TV show or movie as you. These people are 100 feet from your front door, watching the same thing as you—and maybe on a better TV. It doesn't take much effort to invite them over or head over to their place. Just choose to do something with others that you were going to do alone.

We know it's easy to assume that our neighbors don't want to participate in any of these activities with us, but we're consistently surprised at the positive responses we get to invitations. We simply invite people to join in our regular activities, or, conversely, now they invite us into some of their regular activities.

It's also easy to assume that people are too busy to want to join you in some activity. But plenty of people are hungry for interaction, particularly when it's part of an overall picture of a growing friendship. The world around us is lonelier than we know, so it's good to have your radar up, purposefully looking for ways you can engage with people who live close to you. One of the easiest things to do is eat together. So it's easy to say, "You're eating; we're eating; let's eat together." Yes, that does require some intentionality. But it's not hard to invite others to join you because you are already going to eat anyway, right? Just try it. You'll be surprised at how easy it is.

What's more, doing the small things and sharing what you love can often overlap with the actual needs of neighbors. You have some skills that enable you to serve others, just as our friend Robb learned. Here is his story. "I would say that I am friends with most of my neighbors. With almost everyone, I am comfortable enough with our friendship to knock on their garage door instead of the front door. They do the same when they come over to my house. I make my living as a contractor, and this has enabled me to serve some of my neighbors in a very tangible way.

"On our block there are a couple of single moms and an elderly couple. A few years ago, I mentioned to them that I was willing to help out if they needed any home repairs. This has opened up a lot of opportunities for me to connect with others that God has placed around me. Often I will invite one of my other neighbors to come with me when I am tackling a small project in the neighborhood. Not only am I able to use my skills to serve but I also get to know another neighbor better. It has simply been a matter of making myself available and inviting others to join in.

"Last spring my wife and I were thinking about throwing a big block party. As we were in the planning stages, we were trying to come up with some ways to start to get to know our neighbors. One night I decided to make s'mores. It was a beautiful spring evening, and, on a whim, I decided to go around the block and invite people to join us. All but two of our neighbors showed up, and we ended up hanging out around the fire pit for more than two hours. Midway through the evening, it dawned on me that we were actually having a spontaneous block party that required no planning whatsoever! That summer my wife and I decided to look for other simple ways to gather together with our neighbors.

"For instance, one of the single moms on our block has two young children. I try to spend time with them by playing catch or by just hanging out and having fun with them. One afternoon my son found an old electric four-wheeler in a dumpster. It was in rough shape. It had no charger, and the wheels were broken. Someone had obviously thrown it out for a reason. I knew the single mom's youngest son, Noah, had an electric four-wheeler as well, so I figured out a way to charge the piece of junk that my son had brought home. Then I fixed the wheels. Finally, I asked Noah if he would like to take me on in a race in the cul-de-sac.

"We invited all the neighbors to come out and watch. I set up a course with cones, and we played it up like it was the Indy 500. We ended up racing until the batteries were dead! I know that I looked pretty silly sitting on a child's electric four-wheeler, but we still talk about that race nearly ten years later. I have learned that it doesn't take a lot to create memories that last for a long time."

Robb's story is a perfect example of how little things can really make a big difference, as well as the power of using your talents to serve others. The idea seems so simple—just do what you're already doing, invite others to the table, and watch what God does as a result.

This simple concept is freeing in many ways. You're probably already doing this with several people in your life. It doesn't require taking another class or going to another conference or sitting through another seminar. All it requires is that you take a step back, think about things that you already love, and invite your neighbors to join in.

Don't Give Up

When we do simple things over time, we can make a big impact. At first, it probably won't feel as if you are doing anything monumental. In fact, if done correctly, it probably won't feel that interesting at all. Keep in mind, though, that most of the changes that take place in our lives don't come through one huge moment. Our body changes slowly. Our families change slowly. Our friendships change slowly. Sure, there can be huge breakthroughs or setbacks at any moment, but the majority of lasting change in our lives comes through consistent, regular investment. The challenge is to simply make those small investments, stay in the game, and share your day-to-day life with those around you. And then don't give up.

This message is illustrated perfectly in one of baseball's most memorable moments. On September 6, 1995, at Camden Yards in Baltimore, the Baltimore Orioles and California Angels played an unforgettable game. The Orioles won it 4 to 2, but that's not what made the game unforgettable. The sellout crowd in Baltimore and the millions of people who saw the game live on television had the opportunity to witness one of the truly remarkable achievements in the history of sports.

On that night in September 1995, Cal Ripken Jr. played in his 2,131st consecutive game, breaking one of the most unattainable records in baseball history—Lou Gehrig's 2,130 consecutive-games-played streak, which stood for fifty-six years. Ripken was the one to finally beat it.

The biggest outpouring of emotion came after the fifth inning when the game became official. The crowd didn't stop cheering for more than twenty-two minutes! They weren't cheering for someone who hit the most home runs of all time or had the highest career batting average or who had just thrown a perfect game. Ripken was celebrated wildly for twenty-two minutes, not for a single athletic achievement but rather for an achievement of endurance. For fourteen straight years, playing in every single game of every single season, Ripken simply showed up and did his job. And on that night, sports fans everywhere passionately recognized what he had accomplished.

That fifth inning must have been an amazing scene to witness from the stands. The members of the Orioles bull pen jogged in from left field, and the crowd's roar became deafening when the huge illuminated numbers hanging on the warehouse beyond the right-field wall were flipped to 2,131. A salute of fireworks lit up the sky.

Ripken alternated between sitting in the Orioles dugout and being shoved onto the field by teammates to take curtain calls, eight in all. He walked over to the seat behind home plate where his wife and his children were seated. He looked up at the box high above the field where his father, Cal Ripken Sr., was watching the game. His dad, this old-school baseball man, was crying.

But the best was yet to come. When Ripken tried to go back into the dugout, his teammates wouldn't let him in. They pushed him out on the field for a victory lap around the field. With forty-six thousand fans screaming themselves hoarse and millions of people at home wiping away the tears, Ripken slowly made his way around the warning track at Camden Yards. He shook hands with the fans, police officers, field attendants, and even the opposing team. It was a thunderous tribute to a man who simply showed up and did his job day after day.

As we learn to become better neighbors, we can learn a lot from Ripken and his commitment to the small things. You'd better believe he was tired. In many of the games he played during that fourteen-year stretch, he had injured his knees, sprained his ankles, and endured common colds like the rest of us. He experienced some prolonged hitting droughts and some real failure and discouragements along the way. In fact, many suggested that he was hurting the team by persisting in his streak. But he never gave up. He never quit.

Remember, it's often the small moments that count, so focus faithfully on the small things day in and day out, and over time change can and will happen. Small things have a way of adding up and producing disproportionately great results.

It's simple: just share what you love to do. Make small steps. Give the little you have and watch God do a miracle.

7

Motives Matter

We want to be clear about something when it comes to the art of neighboring. This is not an evangelism strategy. And if evangelism is your only motive, then you won't be a very good neighbor. However, if neighboring is done with the right posture, then people who don't know God will most certainly come to know him.

Years ago I (Jay) worked in phone sales. Yep, I was a telemarketer. For eight hours a day, I wore a headset, sat in a cubicle, and phoned number after number. It was a brutal job that required determination and thick skin. As you might imagine, many said no as soon as I began to talk. The vast majority either hung up immediately or slammed down the phone with an expletive. I didn't want to be there, but I was broke and I needed to pay bills. Along the way, though, I learned some valuable lessons.

I was charged with trying to sell travel programs. We received numbers gathered from hotel promotions and then worked from a sales script. Once I got someone on the phone, I started my pitch. I had a fantastic one-time offer: For only one dollar up front, a person could buy into the program and then cancel at any time in the next ninety days. All they had to do was provide a credit card number and they would receive vouchers for random items and services. The trick was that I needed to sign the people up for the program, which had a two-hundred-dollar annual fee when the trial period was over. Our hope was that they would sign on and forget about the impending fee. And most people did.

When people said no, our big aim was to quickly answer their every objection. We had a binder in front of us and could flip to various answers, depending on what people said. So if a person said, "Nah, I don't think so. Times are tough right now," I'd flip to the correct tab and say something like, "I totally understand that times are tough, Mr. Smith. But don't you think that one of the best ways of putting money back into your family's checking account is by investing in solid offers such as these?"

Not only would we answer objections, we were taught all the tricks of high-pressure sales—how to create a sense of urgency. *People always needed to decide today. The offer was only good for a limited time. The price would be going up soon. Quantities were limited.* Very simply, we were taught to push for the sale. This was the reason we were in business, wasn't it, to make the sale? ABC—Always Be Closing—was our motto. If someone said no, we tried to keep the person on the line talking. We were trained to answer at least three objections before we were allowed to let the customer go. The goal was to wear people down and close the sale.

While this may not be the most appealing strategy, sales, of course, is a respectable profession. Companies rely on sales teams and approaches like these to sell their products and stay in business.

But as a pastor, I have noticed some striking similarities between the sales industry and how some Christians share their faith. In a well-meaning attempt to "sell" a good thing, we have all heard pastors use high-pressure sales techniques to sell the gospel. "What would happen if you walked out of this room today and were hit by a car and died? Would you go to heaven or hell?"

The core desire behind these questions is actually very honorable. But no one wants to come off like a telemarketer when talking about the most important message that we have to share. Is there another option? Please tell me that there is another way!

Ulterior versus Ultimate

We have both been greatly influenced by the book *To Transform a City* by Eric Swanson and Sam Williams (Zondervan, 2010). In their book, the authors use the phrase "ulterior versus ultimate" to describe common motives in building relationships with others.

> *Ulterior* means something is intentionally kept concealed. An ulterior motive is usually manipulative. It's when we do or say one thing out in the open but intend or mean another thing in private.

Ultimate means the farthest point of a journey. An ultimate goal is an eventual point or a longed-for destination. Examples are when a person begins college hoping to become a physician one day or when a kid starts playing basketball with dreams of one day playing in the NBA.

The *ulterior* motive in good neighboring must never be to share the gospel.

But the *ultimate* motive is just that—to share the story of Jesus and his impact on our lives.

There's a big difference. The "agenda" we need to drop is the well-meaning tendency to be friends with people for the sole purpose of converting them to our faith. Many so desperately want to move people forward spiritually that they push them according to their timetable, not according to how God is working in them. It's tempting to offer friendship with strings attached.

We want to be clear. None of those motives are bad in and of themselves. We believe strongly that making a decision to enter into a relationship with God through his Son Jesus is the most important decision anyone can make. We believe that Jesus provides real solutions for people and that orienting our lives around him is the best way to live. We believe that Jesus answers the ultimate questions of life and has the ultimate answers for our cities and neighborhoods. Our hope, dream, and desire is that everyone will have a meaningful relationship with Jesus. So sharing the story of Jesus and his impact on our lives is the right motive, but it cannot be an ulterior motive in developing relationships. We don't love our neighbors to convert them; we love our neighbors because we are converted.

And the truth is, many Christians have been taught by well-meaning people that they should do nice things solely for an opportunity to have a spiritual conversation. But Jesus never called us to use a bait-and-switch approach, where we become friends with people *only* to share spiritual truths with them. We are called to love people—period. Whether those people ever take any steps toward God is beside the point. We are called to love our neighbors unconditionally, without expecting anything in return. The Great Commandment says, "Love your neighbor as yourself." The commandment ends there, with no other expectations given. Thus good neighboring is an end in itself.

The difference between ulterior and ultimate motives involves much more than semantics, and the bait-and-switch paradigm for evangelism is probably ingrained into our thinking more deeply than we realize. Most believers want the people they know to have an authentic relationship with Jesus. But if our friends choose not to enter into that relationship, we should still desire to be friends with them. Obviously we shouldn't cut someone loose because he or she isn't interested in Jesus.

So the questions arise: When it comes to neighboring, how do we best share our faith in Jesus? When do we share our faith? And what kind of posture should we take when it comes to spiritual matters?

Door to Door

Danielle and I (Jay) wanted to throw a block party to connect with our neighbors. Some of them joined us in planning it, and before we knew it, we had a plan. As the date for the party approached, Danielle and I printed up some flyers. We rounded up our daughters and spent a weekend afternoon going door-to-door, inviting neighbors. We already knew the neighbors closest to us were attending, so we cast a wider net and invited the rest of the block.

As we were walking through the neighborhood, we ran into some Jehovah's Witnesses who were knocking on doors as well. With pamphlets in hand, they passed by us, and it was clear that they had been to many of the same houses we were visiting. So it wasn't surprising that no one came to the door at many of the homes. We knew there were people inside, but maybe they thought we were the other guys doubling back for another religious pitch. It felt awkward to stuff our block party flyer alongside Jehovah's Witness pamphlets, but we wanted to make sure that all the neighbors were invited.

Walking a bit farther, we bumped into a neighbor we hadn't met before. After exchanging some chitchat, he asked if he could give our girls a present. I looked awkwardly at Danielle and then asked what it was. He said it was a surprise. That made me nervous. I don't normally allow strange people to give gifts to my kids. But we were trying to be good neighbors, so I shrugged and nodded.

He smiled, went and got something out of his car, and came back. He handed my two girls a strange-looking little box and explained that each side of the cube showed them the steps of how to start a new relationship with God. He proceeded to demonstrate what we later learned is an EvangeCube. It resembles a Rubik's Cube, but as you open and close it, you can share with someone about how Jesus died and rose again.

I stood in awkward silence. A little later, I finally told him I was a pastor (also awkward). I was embarrassed that I didn't know this neighbor, even though he lived just four houses away from us, and he had no idea that I was a pastor. So much was revealed in that short encounter. Apparently this is what this guy does. He shares his faith without even knowing who he's talking to. I doubt he would have done that if he knew I was a pastor. There was a lot wrong with that moment.

Walking a bit farther, we bumped into another guy and invited him to the block party. He asked why we were having one.

"We want the neighborhood to be more connected," I said. "We know that most people feel isolated and really want to get to know each other. We also know that as we all get to know each other, it makes the neighborhood safer."

He seemed interested, so I shared that we were looking forward to doing this because a bunch of other neighborhoods in our community were having block parties as well. I went on to tell him that our mayor was really excited about this neighborhood initiative and about how churches all over our city were encouraging their people to become better neighbors.

Then he asked me what I did for a living. Now, for those of you pastors out there, you know how this goes. And for those of you who aren't pastors, let me tell you that what happened next is typical.

When I told him I was a pastor, he suddenly stiffened up and began to act very strange. I tried my best to joke around so he would relax, but it was obvious that my being a pastor made him uncomfortable. Was he uncomfortable only because I was a pastor? Or perhaps it was because I told him about the church initiative to encourage good neighboring. Was he afraid I was just trying to trick him into some kind of a spiritual conversation? Was I coming off like the guy with the EvangeCube or like the door-to-door Jehovah's Witnesses? Now I was the one feeling weird.

Walking home that day, I was suddenly aware of all the different ways people share their faith and how threatening it can appear to others. After all, people who go door-to-door "selling" religion tend to be perceived as pushy and annoying. When strangers use little boxes to describe the incredible story of Jesus, it can be awkward, especially when you don't even know who they are. I have no doubt that these people had good, pure intentions, but surely there's a better way. And more important, was I doing anything different as a neighbor? How should I be sharing my faith as a good neighbor?

When we take Jesus seriously, we really do want to share with others what we love, what we enjoy, what we believe. The challenge, though, is *how*. Remember, we don't want to come off as preachy or force our beliefs down others' throats. Those who have been targeted in the past are wary. So when the topic of religion comes up, they simply leave the room or shut down altogether. And that is the last thing we want to do while developing relationships.

Learning to Share Your Story

Often Christians struggle with how best to share their faith. They clam up because they don't know what to say or how to say it. Or they push forward and alienate themselves. They so fervently want people to believe what they believe that they are willing to shift into high-pressure mode. It's like they're trying to strong-arm people into heaven.

But we believe there is a different way. When people are in relationship with others, they naturally share what they love. For instance, I (Jay) love golf. If you are around me for any significant amount of time, we will most likely end up talking about golf at some point. And this principle is true for everyone. When we are around people for any amount of time, we begin to share with them the things we love.

If you love Jesus, then he will naturally come up in your conversations. It happens as we share the substance of who we are. So the more you love Jesus, the more that love will be apparent in your conversations and relationships. Conversely, if you find that you aren't talking about Jesus with those around you, perhaps you don't have a very good relationship with those people. Or it might mean you don't have a very deep relationship with Jesus. Or perhaps you are simply afraid of how you will be perceived.

For some, it can be scary to share their true beliefs, religious or otherwise. If this is the case, we'd like to encourage you to overcome those fears.

Your life is a story—whether you realize it or not. So how would you tell it to someone else? What are the different layers in your story? And what parts are you most afraid to tell? Sharing your story, both the good and bad parts, is key to building long-lasting relationships.

God teaches us this firsthand through the Bible. He doesn't offer lists of dos and don'ts to relay his message. Rather, the stories in the Bible help illustrate how he has chosen to interact with people over time. And in reading his story, we get a sense of who he is and what he is like. We begin to understand that he longs to be in relationship with us. We begin to recognize his movement in our lives as we become familiar with how God interacted in the lives of others in the Bible.

We need to recognize that every single one of our neighbors has a story as well. Deep down we all want to share our story. We want to feel as though our story connects to something larger than ourselves. As we learn to hear others' stories, we can connect to their heart and see how God is at work in their lives.

It's about authenticity. It's honestly talking about how your walk with Jesus makes a difference. Your story should reflect not only your life before your encounter with Jesus, but also what your life has been like after your newfound relationship with him. Those around us need to hear how someone's faith in Jesus has made a world of difference.

God's story isn't forced; if you have a relationship with Jesus, he is living out his story through you. And once you have a clear sense of how God is moving in your life, you have an active way to share your faith. It won't be a canned sales pitch, but rather a powerful demonstration of God's activity in your life now.

Just as important, we must learn how to listen to our neighbors' stories. When we are neighboring well, this will happen in a natural way. We won't need to press them. Be available to enter into meaningful conversations with your neighbors, and God will open the door to further opportunity.

What does a friendly and ever-deepening conversation look like? We've noticed a pattern that often takes place over time. Conversations follow this pattern: first we talk about the things we can see, then basic personal information, later our dreams and desires, and after some time our regrets, losses, and pain.

The Things We Can See

Early on in relationships, we talk with our neighbors about the things we both can see—the weather, the crazy color of a neighbor's house, the increased traffic on our street, to name a few. We rarely enter into conversations of depth with someone we have just met.

Basic Personal Information

As we begin to get to know people, we begin to talk about basic information. Questions go both ways, such as:

How long have you lived here?
Where did you grow up?
What do you do for a living?
Are you married? How long?
Where did you guys meet?
Do you have kids?

These are basic facts that people are usually willing to share. Then as you learn about their story, you will naturally end up noticing things that you share in common.

Our Dreams and Desires

As we get to know people over time, we will share our hopes and dreams with one another. All of us have dreams of what we might become or hope to achieve. So it's helpful to ask questions that allow others to share their personal goals and aspirations. For example, you might ask:

What do you love most about what you do?

If you could do anything, what would you do?

Our Regrets, Losses, and Pain

As we grow close to people, we have opportunities to share about some of our regrets or painful experiences. To some degree or another we have all experienced pain, and often it is our pain that shapes us the most. As we share our difficult experiences with others and how we are coping (or not coping), we create a safe environment in which others can share their pain.

It's true that most people are reticent about sharing such information with others. But after a relationship has begun and you show genuine interest, you will be surprised at what people will share. Often people want to talk about the loss of someone they love, a hard relationship, or a challenging job situation. When we get authentic and honest, we create an avenue for our friends to do the same.

As we start to interact with people in these deeper places, we will be able to share the things that are most important to us. And if you have a deep, personal relationship with Jesus, he will be a big part of your story. Our dreams, desires, and pains are intertwined with our relationship with God. When we show where our story overlaps with our neighbor's story, and with God's story, then our neighbors might start wondering if their story might join God's as well.

But is that really enough? Is loving our neighbor and looking for ways to share our story all that we are commanded to do? What about the Great Commission? You know, Jesus's command to make disciples of all the nations.

The Two Greats

It's important for us to think about and understand how the Great Commission relates to all we have said about the Great Commandment. The Great Commission is found in Matthew 28, and the part that most of us are familiar with is found in verses 19–20: "Therefore go and make disciples of all nations, baptizing them in the name of the Father and of the Son and of the Holy Spirit, and teaching them to obey everything I have commanded you."

The Great Commandment, as mentioned, is found in a number of places in the Bible. One instance is Luke 10:27, where it is quoted by a man of the law in a conversation that he had with Jesus: "'Love the Lord your God with all your heart and with all your soul and with all your strength and with all your mind'; and, 'Love your neighbor as yourself.'"

If we live out the Great Commandment, an environment is created where the Great Commission can be effectively obeyed. Loving people who live around us fosters an environment where people trust one another. Chances are most people who don't believe in God have had at least one negative experience with religion. For them, to enter into a spiritual conversation can be uncomfortable, unpalatable, unappealing, and perhaps even feel threatening.

People are suspicious of those who have a message that doesn't align with what they have experienced. This kind of inconsistency can lead to perceptions of phoniness, ultimately hindering any hope of a real relationship. We are all tired of the telemarketers interrupting dinner and salesmen who will say anything to make us believe we can't live without the product they are selling. We've been duped in the past and have learned to be suspicious of slick-talking strangers trying to sell us something. Marketing is so prevalent in our culture that we've learned to put up barriers.

However, when we truly take the Great Commandment seriously, we become credible messengers who bring a message evidenced in both word and deed. As we love those around us, we represent the kind of life Jesus wants us to live: the "full life" that Jesus describes in John 10:10. When we share our lives and our story, our neighbors have a chance to see who we really are. They know we aren't perfect but they can see how our faith affects how we do life with others. We fulfill the words of Jesus in Matthew 5:14–16:

> You are the light of the world. A town built on a hill cannot be hidden. Neither do people light a lamp and put it under a bowl. Instead they put it on its stand, and it gives light to everyone in the house. In the same way, let your light shine before others, that they may see your good deeds and glorify your Father in heaven.

Jesus is declaring that we can live in such a way that people around us will look to God because of how we are living. When they see us living out a life of love, they will actually be seeing God in us. They may not even know who God is, but they will start to be curious because of the way we live out our lives.

We believe that Jesus offers us the best kind of life and that we should do what he commands, not just because we have to but because we want to, not just because it's best for us but because it's also good for others. Jesus isn't just trying to make moral people. We can trust that he offers us a way of life that is simply better than any other.

Trust and Obey

Before we start talking to others about Jesus in our endeavor to become better neighbors, it's important that we examine our own lives and our relationship with him. Are we truly walking in obedience to the clear commands of Jesus, particularly, the one he says sums up all the rest—the Great Commandment?

The Great Commandment is a matter of obedience to those who know and follow Jesus. We don't love our neighbors so they will know Jesus; we love our neighbors because we already love Jesus and trust him. We are called to love our neighbors, even if our neighbors never show any interest in Jesus, because we have made Jesus our highest priority. Again, we are not supposed to love our neighbors to convert them. We love our neighbors because we have been converted. To put it even more bluntly, we don't love people so they will believe what we believe. Many people we love and serve won't ever believe, and that's okay. We just love our neighbors. That's it.

And as we love them, from time to time, we will talk to them about what is most important in our lives. We don't just share the toys we have or the hobbies we enjoy. We share about the deeper parts of our heart. When we love Jesus, we share that with others because we love them. We love them enough to share the vulnerable parts of our life, and that includes our faith in Jesus. We believe this is the most effective way to share our faith.

When you love God and love other people, deep spiritual things transpire. You don't need to worry about what will happen when you attempt to become a good neighbor. You don't need to be anxious about the structure or strategy of what happens. You just need to be faithful and flexible.

Our friend Mark told us his story of neighboring well. Notice in his story how small things mattered. Sometimes they led to bigger things; sometimes they didn't. Mark wrote: "I'd say our neighborhood is different from a year ago. We ended up having a block party. It was weird knocking on doors of people I didn't know. I felt like a kid selling Cub Scout popcorn again. Everyone was really kind of timid; they weren't sure if they wanted to sign up at first. I asked everyone to bring something. It was odd saying, 'Hey, you don't know me, but I need to know what you're going to bring to our block party.' Everyone was a good sport, though. I think most everyone showed up.

"The summer was great. Some of our relationships stayed the same; some of them got a little deeper. In particular, one couple was heading into a rough place in their marriage. While we were already friends with them, although merely on a surface level, the block party sparked a deeper connection. I can just say that God really allowed us to help them in a couple of ways. We prayed for them a lot. We tried to tell them that we thought God could help them through. We didn't want to be pushy, but we wanted them to know about how God strengthened our marriage and how he could help their marriage as well.

"We were able to be with them in a tough time when their marriage may not have made it. They wanted to save their marriage and were so authentic and real with us. They even started attending a church with someone they trusted. The husband, Ron, told me last week that he prayed for *me*. Wow. I'm not sure, but that seems like God is at work in and around us. It's pretty special to see God's kingdom really break out.

"People who live on our street seem to know each other now. I'm sure there will still be rifts, new neighbors, unkempt yards, fireworks for the entire month of June, and some inconsiderate guy who fires up his dirt bike early on a Saturday morning. But I would encourage anybody to go knock on a door and try to talk to someone. Just share a little about yourself. Things will be messy, but Jesus brings hope. You'll get more out of it than some new people to borrow tools from or who can babysit your kid. God actually might want to do something through those relationships, maybe with them, maybe with you."

What Mark did was really simple. There was no great initiative, no tension over what he would say. Yes, it did require some guts to go around and invite a bunch of neighbors who didn't know each other to a block party. Yes, he did go the extra mile and enter into the mess of his neighbors' difficult marriage. He did pray for them often and told them he thought God could help them through it. He shared about how God worked in his marriage. But there was no eloquent speech, no canned program, no brochures or complexity involved. He just got involved and shared his story with them. He offered them hope when they felt hopeless.

That's really all he did. And good things flowed from there. That's the kind of good neighboring Jesus uses for his purposes.

A Simple Plan

The beauty of the art of neighboring is that it's simple and genuine. You don't need to memorize any pitches. You don't need to chart out a master plan for evangelizing your neighborhood. You don't need to worry about having a canned speech in your back pocket. In short, you need *not* make your neighbors your "pet project"; make them your friends. You simply need to love God with all your heart, soul, mind, strength, and body, and love your neighbor as yourself. When those things happen, everything else falls into place. The goal is to faithfully tell your story, God's story. Then listen to their story and ask God to lead you.

So what should you do when your neighbors begin to ask you about what you believe and why? We want to encourage you to lean into those moments. Is there any wrong move you could make? Probably not. It's easy to want a formula to follow, but we want to encourage you to simply talk about whom you love and why you love him. Be real, speak from your heart, and let God lead the way.

8

The Art of Receiving

Have you ever had a friendship that felt one-sided? One in which all you did was give, give, give? You were constantly helping out, going the extra mile, giving advice, and pouring your energy into someone else. At first it felt great, as though you were truly helping someone in need. This person appreciated your efforts and expressed gratitude. Over time, though, the relationship lacked genuine depth. You grew tired. You felt used. The person was a bottomless pit of needs; there was no way for your friendship to evolve into a satisfying relationship for both of you.

Or maybe you were friends with a person who was always caring for you. As a result, she didn't show any signs of need. She was available to help when you needed it but didn't ever seem to need help in her own life. This person's problem was a lack of vulnerability, and this made you feel like a project and not a participant in the relationship.

Great neighborhoods are built on reciprocal relationships, on two-way streets. At the end of the day, no one wants to feel like a project. We want to feel that we bring something to the table. But when it comes to neighboring well, one of the biggest temptations is to turn neighbors into projects. We put on the "superneighbor cape" and rush out to serve our neighbors and make a difference on our block. This really isn't a bad thing, but if this is all we ever do, then our relationships will be empty. If we don't allow people to meet any of our needs, we limit what God wants to do in our neighborhood and our life.

Allowing ourselves to be on the receiving end can be harder than it looks. Our tendency is to put ourselves in positions of power—in this case, always being the one to give. We want to be seen as the capable one with all the resources and answers. But being in a relationship where we allow others to meet our needs is always a good thing. The art of neighboring involves our being able both to give of our time and energy and, just as important, to receive from others.

"For" or "With"

George and Kate live in a middle-class subdivision. Their neighbor, Heather, is a single mom. Over the past few years, George and Kate have made it a point to be good neighbors to Heather and her son. If her lawn needs to be mowed or if the driveway needs to be shoveled, George will often do it after he's finished his own. If Heather needs someone to share with or vent to, then Kate makes time to listen.

Recently when George and Kate were in their backyard putting mulch around their bushes, they came up a bag short. Heather happened to stop by, and when they told her they were getting ready to go to the store to get more mulch, Heather said, "Hey, I have an extra bag of mulch."

"That's okay," George said. "We can pick one up easy enough. We need to get some other things as well."

"No, I really want you to have it." There was a look of insistence on Heather's face.

Their first reaction was to say no. They didn't want to take a bag of mulch from a single mom. They knew her money was tight and even a bag of mulch had to be carefully budgeted. But Heather was persistent, almost aggressive. Finally, they said yes.

Later when George and Kate talked about it, they understood that, perhaps for the first time, by allowing Heather to give them the bag of mulch, they were allowing her to care for them. In essence she was saying, "You're always helping me out all the time. This is a way of letting me help you back." Really, what they did that day was allow her to be a participant in their relationship. She was saying, "We're participants in this together."

When giving is one-sided, it robs the "needy" one of his dignity, because it makes him dependent. But when giving is two-sided, everyone feels a sense of worth. We need to understand that everyone on our block has something to bring to a relationship.

What's more, good neighboring is *not* about doing charity work. It's not simply about doing for others and looking for ways to give and give and give. Rather, good neighboring is about helping to create a sense of community within your neighborhood. It's about empowering people and breaking down walls. It's about everybody doing something together for the common good. As you might imagine, this is much easier said than done. Receiving can be a challenge for a number of reasons. It takes humility, it may feel wrong to impose on someone else, and it requires vulnerability.

Humility

To receive help requires humility. When we receive something, we are often acknowledging that there is someone who possesses what we don't have. We are admitting that we actually need her help.

We want to be the capable ones who swoop onto the scene and do our good deeds. But when we receive something from somebody else, it forces us to admit we are in need as well. When we allow others to provide for us, we are forced to acknowledge that we are needy. This can be unsettling.

Imposing on Others

From an early age many of us have been taught not to be in another's debt. If someone gives us something, we feel we owe him—we must give something back. We give birthday gifts to those who have gifted us. We pay for lunch this month because our friend paid last month.

And most of us don't like having to ask for someone's help. We don't want to make people go out of their way for us. For example, we'll walk the two miles home rather than ask a friend to drive us.

Perhaps we don't like to depend on others because we feel that it gives them the upper hand. Then they can feel superior because we are in their debt.

Vulnerability

. It takes a certain amount of courage to put ourselves out there and ask another for a favor. What if she turns us down? How embarrassing! What if we find out he's too busy or is having a difficult day, making us feel really insensitive for having asked? We don't want to live with that tension.

Just Admit It

To receive might be easier than you think. It just takes a simple step forward, a willingness to admit that you aren't as good as your neighbor at something or you don't always have everything you need. But no one is going to find fault with you for having a need. Receiving boils down to simply admitting your need and asking for help.

For example, in addition to my ineptitude with cars, I (Dave) would also be considered inept as a handyman. So I judge the effectiveness of each project by two things. Did I actually finish the task, and how many trips to Home Depot did it take for me to complete said task? Usually I consider anything under four trips a success.

A couple of years ago, my wife pointed out to me that there was something wrong with the step leading from the garage into the house. It was starting to come loose, and every time someone stepped on it, it gave a little bit. Basically it was a sprained ankle waiting to happen.

About six months after learning it was broken, I happened to be hanging out in my neighbor's garage and noticed the beautiful steps into his house. I asked Don about them. When he said he had made the steps himself, I thought immediately that I could use his help.

I asked Don if he would come over, look at my step, and give me some advice on how best to fix it. We walked across the street. After taking one glance, he told me that we could easily fix it in less than thirty minutes.

The next thing I knew, my neighbor and I were sitting on the floor of my garage. He was building a new step and attaching it to my house. I was handing him tools and grabbing us some drinks. Half an hour later, I had a new step that wasn't a death trap and I still had the majority of my Saturday left to do other things.

What happened that day between my neighbor and me was an act of good neighboring—on *my* part, as well as on his. He helped me out, we had an opportunity to spend a little time together, and at the end of the day, I was able to cross something off my "honey do" list.

The key to making it all happen was that I asked for his advice and his help.

Don't Force It

Authenticity is crucial when it comes to the art of receiving. As you begin to look for ways to receive, you might be tempted to create artificial situations so you can interact with your neighbors. You might find yourself thinking, *I haven't seen Karen in a while. I don't really need any sugar right now but maybe I should just go over to her house and ask to borrow some.*

This is actually a stupid idea. For starters, it lacks integrity and it is dishonest. If our goal is to model a different way of living to those who live around us, we must strive to be above board with our motives. What's more, most people can see through well-meaning but manufactured attempts at interaction.

Instead, the construction of a two-way street works best when there's genuine need. If you're baking a pie and run out of sugar, then by all means go over to your neighbor's house and ask to borrow some. But don't make up fictional reasons for knocking on her door.

Frankly, we believe that borrowing something from your neighbor is a lost art. These days if a person runs out of something, it feels much more natural to jump in the car and head down to the corner store to get it. But it wasn't always that way. It used to be that neighbors had an understanding among themselves. If something was needed, it was perfectly acceptable to go next door and borrow some milk, eggs, a rake, or a snowblower, whatever was needed. We believe that part of being a good neighbor means returning to those days of depending on and helping one another.

So the next time you genuinely need something in a hurry, go next door and ask to borrow it. Perhaps you'll get a funny look. But more often than not, your neighbor will be happy and willing to oblige. When a community of reciprocity is created, there are real opportunities to serve and be served. Then a neighborhood becomes less isolated and more self-sufficient as a whole. A feeling of "We can do this together" is created, and that's healthy.

Keep in mind that a bond is created any time someone serves you, or whenever you serve someone else. If you help a neighbor shovel her driveway, you feel closer to that neighbor. If a neighbor loans you his truck to go pick up a Ping-Pong table, you create a bond.

The results of receiving can be huge, as Claire shares. "Recently my husband went to the hospital for surgery. It wasn't serious, just an afternoon procedure. But in the end, it meant he was out of commission for several days while he recuperated. It was surprising how much additional work was created around the house during this time.

"On the day of the surgery, someone needed to drive my husband back from the hospital, then do the same the next day (both to and from the hospital), so he could get his bandages removed. We have a two-year-old son and a three-and-a half-year-old daughter, and they both still nap in the afternoon. I felt that I needed to be in two places at one time and was stressed about what I was going to do.

"Fortunately, I was friendly with another young mom with two children who lives just across the street from us. When I mentioned the surgery, she gave me the typical auto reply, 'Let me know if there is anything I can do.'

"I was tempted to let her offer go, as I really don't like to ask for help. However, I stopped myself and said, 'Actually, is there any way that you could watch my two kids for a few hours on Monday and Tuesday?' I really didn't want to impose on her. I am well aware of how hard it is to take care of two kids, much less four.

"But it turned out to be a great decision. There is no way I could have looked after my husband and my kids during those first two days. It was hectic, and I am grateful that I had a neighbor I could count on.

"More important, a strong bond was forged between my neighbor and me as a result of her being there when I was in need. Since that moment, we are much closer, even though we haven't really spent any more time together than before the incident.

"It's dawned on me that the most important thing I've ever done to further our relationship was to allow her to care for our family."

An Act of Receiving

In Luke 7 one of the Pharisees invited Jesus to have dinner with him. While there, a woman described as having "lived a sinful life in that town" (translation: she was a prostitute) learned that Jesus was at the house. She brought an expensive alabaster jar of perfume, poured it out on Jesus's feet, and wiped his feet with her hair. She took the only thing she had of value and used it to worship Jesus. The perfume was expensive, and undoubtedly she had used it to attract men. She poured the perfume on Jesus in the middle of a party, perhaps making her and Jesus feel very vulnerable and even in danger, since there were important religious men in attendance. If Jesus had rejected her offering, it would have crushed her.

But he didn't. He actually went so far as to defend her and said that the way she was worshiping rivaled the worship of the religious leaders present in the room.

I doubt that Jesus was in great need of a foot washing and a special perfume treatment. It wasn't his need at that party at that time, but it was what the woman had to offer him. In fact, it was all she had. And he received it willingly because he knew that his willingness to receive this gift meant everything to her. It meant that she could have dignity in her worship and that her gift counted. He received her gift even though others in the room found it inappropriate and excessive.

Jesus chose to make himself vulnerable. The one who came to give everything for us was also willing to receive from us. Yes, Jesus practiced the art of receiving.

The art of receiving is not complicated. It comes down to being aware of our own needs. It's about opening our eyes, then being vulnerable enough to ask and receive. After all, you couldn't possibly possess all the skills, resources, or tools you need, right? So acknowledge your needs and start noticing the people in your neighborhood who might be willing to help.

9

The Art of Setting Boundaries

As you begin getting in touch with the needs of those around you, you are going to encounter the real-life issues of some of your neighbors. You are going to be reminded of the reasons most people avoid entering into relationship with those who live nearest to them. In short, at times it can feel overwhelming to be in real relationships with our neighbors. You may start to wonder, *What have those guys gotten me into?* Rick's story sheds some light on this.

The friendship started out innocently enough. Rick first met his neighbor Kurt one day while they were both working on their lawns. Rick's wife baked some cookies for Kurt and his wife. Nothing big. They were nice enough people. Rick had noticed that they had their share of difficulties in their relationship but nothing huge.

One evening Kurt knocked on Rick's door and said he and his wife had been arguing. He asked if there was any way he could crash at their place for the night. Rick's heart went out to him. Of course, he'd give him some help in a time of crisis.

That first night on Rick's couch stretched into another night and then another night. Then a week. Then two weeks. Rick and his wife felt stuck.

At one point, realizing that this was going to be a longer commitment than he had anticipated, Rick decided to give Kurt a key so he could come and go as needed. Rick and his wife kept telling each other, "Surely this is just a rough patch in their marriage. Kurt's not bothering us. He's just using the couch in the basement."

And sure enough, things did seem to get better. After about a month, Kurt and his wife patched things up. Kurt moved off their couch and went back home to his wife.

Two months later, however, Rick woke up in the middle of the night to hear a scratching sound downstairs. The front door creaked open on its hinges then closed quietly. He heard footsteps across the linoleum. Someone was in the house. Rick slowly walked down the steps, golf club in hand.

"Hey dude," came a familiar voice. "I was trying not to wake you. We had another fight. Is it cool if I crash on your couch again for a few days?"

Kurt had let himself into the house with the key Rick had given him earlier. This time, apparently, Kurt assumed he was welcome to stay. Rick mumbled something about talking it through in the morning, then stumbled back up the stairs to bed. All he had ever wanted to be was a good neighbor but now he was smack-dab in the middle of a marriage gone bad. His neighbor had a key to his home and was using it to come and go at will. *I am definitely not equipped to do this,* he thought. *This is not what I bargained for.*

Rick started out the process wanting to help Kurt, but clearly something had gone wrong. Is it possible that he had done more damage than good, that by giving Kurt a private suite in the basement, he had actually enabled Kurt and made his situation worse?

Embracing the Mess

When you choose to take the Great Commandment seriously, you become involved with people you might not choose otherwise. Of course some of these people will be people with real problems. Their stories can sometimes be hard and painful; they have difficulties that you would perhaps be tempted to ignore or overlook. But God has given your neighbors to you, and he can use them to change your life.

It's no secret that when our lives become entwined with others' lives, it's natural for problems to surface. Boundaries can get crossed. Expectations can go unspoken or unmet. Anger and misunderstanding can emerge. And somewhere along the line, things may need to be clarified as to what you will—and won't—do to help out a neighbor.

So keep in mind some of these potential pitfalls of being a good neighbor.

Difficult Crises

When you first meet your neighbors, you see only what's on the surface of their lives. Often everything appears normal. The lawn is mowed. The bills are paid. The kids are fed. But as time goes by and you get to know your neighbors, you begin to learn more about what's going on below the surface. That's when it gets interesting. You begin to learn more than you wanted to know, and you often start to feel responsible.

Neediness

Have you ever been in a relationship where things started out well, but pretty soon you realized that the person just wanted to talk to someone, *anyone*? In fact, most of your interactions consisted of her talking on and on. It felt like it would never stop.

One of the challenges with good neighboring is that your neighbors are always there. If a problem arises, you are simply forty feet away. The exciting and scary part of neighboring, though, is that once you jump in, you're in it for the long haul. When things get difficult, there's nowhere to run unless you plan to sell your house.

Dependence

When we neighbor well, we will get to know all the neighbors who live around us, so we will encounter emotionally wounded people. Such people live with unresolved pain and have a limited network of relationships, so they have no one with whom to process their concerns. Their family isn't available or doesn't live in town. They have co-workers, but they're all at the office. Basically, they have limited friendships outside of work and they're not involved in a church.

So whom do they turn to for help? They turn to you if you've made yourself available to listen. Often you are their first and last option. Think about it: in our culture many people have few places to share their deepest dreams and struggles. So when a good neighbor comes along and offers them an opportunity to talk, they let it all come out. You actually care, and that's what they have needed. In situations like these, there is real potential for your life to become intertwined with theirs. Sometimes this is healthy but often it becomes unhealthy.

So when you find yourself in an unhealthy neighboring relationship, you need to take a step back and set some boundaries.

The Difference between *To* and *For*

In all relationships there need to be boundaries. Doctors Henry Cloud and John Townsend wrote an excellent book a few years back called *Boundaries*. We'd encourage you to read this book for a more in-depth look at the subject. Their guidelines can be very helpful when it comes to neighboring. Cloud and Townsend write:

> Boundaries define us. They define *what is me* and *what is not me*. A boundary shows me where I end and someone else begins, leading me to a sense of ownership.
>
> Knowing what I am to own and take responsibility for gives me freedom. If I know where my yard begins and ends, I am free to do with it what I like. Taking responsibility for

my life opens up many different options. However, if I do not "own" my life, my choices and options become very limited.[4]

Think of a boundary as a personal property line. It becomes the fence that divides the things for which we are responsible from the things for which we are not. Boundaries define the terms of what's allowable or not in any relationship. When we love God and want to do the right thing, it can be easy for us to forget our own limits. But it is important to establish the norms and expectations in relationships.

Think of a boundary as the difference between being . . .

responsible *to* a person

and

responsible *for* a person

The distinction between the two little words—*to* and *for*—may seem like a small nuance. But actually the distinction constitutes a big difference in how we relate to people.

Being responsible *to* people is healthy. It means we are responsible . . .

to love them

to encourage them

to bless them

to pray for them

to serve them

But being responsible *for* people is unhealthy. In this case, it means we mistakenly take responsibility . . .

for their well-being

for their finances

for their happiness

for their success or failure

for their spiritual progress

for the strength of their marriage

and so on

There is a vital difference between responsibility *to* and responsibility *for* someone. We are responsible to love, to encourage, to bless, to pray, and to help. But we are not responsible for outcomes, for consequences, for emotions, for reactions, for feelings, or for someone else's choices.

It's the difference between being put on the hook to provide a solution and helping a person find a solution for himself or herself. On one hand we can mistakenly set up a giver-receiver mentality, which seldom helps anybody in the long term. On the other hand, we can set up an environment of healthy participation. Clearly that's a better way to go.

Recently our friend Kyle shared a story of how he walked through a delicate scenario with his neighbor. He had built a strong mentoring relationship with a college-age kid in his neighborhood. A few years ago this kid got high, got hungry, and went for a drive. He was busted for a DUI and lost his license and his car. A year later he got his license back but he needed to get another car. His mom was a single parent, and money was tight. So he approached Kyle, asking for help.

The simple solution in a case like this would be for a good neighbor to whip out a checkbook and write a check. Right?

That's what some may think is the answer. The formula becomes: someone in need approaches you; you immediately give him what he needs.

Now in some cases, writing a check can, indeed, be a good solution. Of course that would be appropriate if someone from a reputable charity or international relief agency made an appeal to you for funds. However, in this case, Kyle didn't have the means to do this nor did he think it the best way to actually help this young man. So Kyle went to the boy's mother and asked her what she thought of the situation. She said all she wanted was for her son to get a job and stop getting high. But the major obstacle to his getting a job was transportation. Then Kyle sat down with the young man to see if he really wanted to change. He said he did.

It happened that Kyle had an extra car (nothing special, but at least drivable), and he thought God was challenging him to consider how he could help his neighbor. So he sold the car to the young man's mother for half its resale value. Rather than just giving the kid money and providing him free access to a vehicle, Kyle empowered the mom to provide a means of transportation so her son could work and begin to get back on his feet again.

Fortunately, the kid has since gotten his act together and, ultimately, it was a neighboring success story. But the end result didn't have a lot to do with Kyle. The kid could have just as easily continued smoking weed and lost his new job, regardless of Kyle's car.

It's a good lesson. We are not accountable for the results of our giving. The idea is simply to help people get back in charge of their own lives, not to rescue them.

Giving a Hand versus a Handout

Good neighboring involves living out the distinction between enabling and empowerment. It's the difference between giving a hand and giving a handout. You want others to take responsibility for their own lives, so you can't just hand them solutions with a smile and a handshake. Good neighboring is not about blindly giving handouts. Rather, it means you walk alongside those in need and help them find their way.

The story of the good Samaritan has a lot to teach us about this concept. And while it's a story most of us have thought about more than once, let's look at it from the angle of setting boundaries.

In this parable, found in Luke 10, we read about a man traveling from Jerusalem to Jericho. Thugs attacked him. He was robbed and beaten up and left for dead. Two religious people passed by but they were too busy to get involved, or at least that's what they thought. Finally, a Samaritan stopped and helped the man. The Samaritan bandaged up the man, loaded him on his donkey, and took him to an inn where he could recover.

It's important to note that the good Samaritan continued his trip at this point. One could argue that the good Samaritan should have done more, should have stayed and helped the man further. The Samaritan should have brought the beaten man back to his home, canceled the plans for his own trip, and drastically rearranged his schedule.

But that's not how the story goes. He did some incredible things but not everything. He picked the guy up off the road, took him to an inn, and paid for him to be cared for there. And that was as far as he went. The good Samaritan was willing to be inconvenienced but didn't allow this event to change his entire life.

I (Dave) encountered a similar situation in my neighborhood with an out-of-work truck driver. Every time we talked, he mentioned that the job market was brutal, that his bills were stacking up, and that he feared losing his house. Everything in the conversation led up to the place where I sensed that he wanted to ask for money, although he never did. This man seemed motivated; he seemed to have a real desire to work. He was a good neighbor with a good heart.

I wrestled with how to help him. My wife and I thought about giving him some money to help make ends meet, but it occurred to us that a month later he might still be in the same place. I knew that giving him money would only be a temporary stopgap to his problem anyway. What this man really needed was a job.

So I went and talked to some guys I knew who had connections in the trucking industry. I put together a list of contacts and called them first to explain the situation. A couple of them said they would welcome a call from my neighbor and grant him an interview. Basically I wanted to put the ball back into my neighbor's court.

I took the list of contact numbers over to him. He was surprised and grateful that I had made the effort but he never called anyone on the list. I have no idea why he didn't pursue any of those opportunities but I felt that I had done the right thing by giving him a chance to pursue it on his own. It wasn't my responsibility that he never followed up with any of them. I tried to help but I didn't do everything. I was willing to be inconvenienced but only so far. I wanted to make sure he took responsibility for his own life.

I'd like to think that our friendship was strengthened through the process. We still keep in touch. He's never asked me for money or help since. A few months later he got a job in a different field, so maybe he didn't need to use those contacts after all.

Some people will argue that I could have done more to help my neighbor. I could have opened my checkbook and written the man a check. I could have made the calls for him or tried to get him an interview. That could have been a good way to go. But I believe that in this case, I did the right thing. I didn't force him to do something he didn't want to do. I simply tried to help him get a job; the rest was up to him.

Called to Love

It's reassuring to know that Jesus himself set boundaries with the people he encountered. Often he didn't help people in the way they wanted to be helped. He cured some people but not others. He stopped and talked with some but not all. Sometimes when the crowds were seeking him, he purposely left them and walked the other way, alone. Jesus was not afraid to draw a line, to put responsibility back onto others, which would help them in lasting ways.

When you set a boundary with a neighbor, it's easy to second-guess yourself. You ask things like:

- Have I done enough?
- Could I have done more?

- Am I doing too much?
- Is there something else I should be doing right now?

If you've ever asked yourself questions like these when it comes to good neighboring, you're not alone. We've asked them too. You have to remember what Jesus says. This *is* the best way to live life. When we love God and love our neighbors, we are living the way Jesus intends for us. Sometimes we may feel overwhelmed. We wonder how we ever got ourselves into the situation we're in and we wonder if we've done the right thing.

As we've seen, you can always do more, but it's best to empower others to move forward. My wife, Danielle, and I (Jay) encountered a situation with a neighbor when we had to do exactly that. A few houses down lived a single mom with a high school–age daughter. One day the daughter missed the bus to school. The mom called Danielle from work and asked if there was any way Danielle could take her daughter to school. Sure, it was a bit inconvenient, but Danielle said yes. She piled our two young children in our car and drove the girl to school.

A week later the daughter missed the bus again. Again, the mother called from work and asked us if we could take her to school. This time Danielle asked a simple question, "What happened?"

"Oh," said the mom, "she got up late."

"Well, I probably can't do this a lot," Danielle said. "But I will help one more time."

A month later, we got another call from the mom. This time the daughter had been in a fight at school. It was noon.

The mom wanted to know if Danielle could go pick her up at the principal's office. (The mom couldn't get her until four o'clock.) This time it was inconvenient for Danielle for a lot of reasons, including the interruption of our young children's naptimes. But Danielle said yes with one caveat: only if the four of us would sit down together and talk about their transportation problem.

We went over to their house a day or so later. Our tone was really calm. Truly we weren't angry or annoyed. We told the family we loved them but wondered if there was a better long-term solution rather than Danielle being their default chauffeur.

The girl was old enough to drive, but the mom said she couldn't afford another car for the family. Danielle offered to help the girl get a job so she could begin saving up for her own car. Both the mother and daughter agreed. But a few days later when we asked the girl about it, she admitted she hadn't turned in any applications, nor was she really motivated to do so.

My wife and I had a long conversation about what we should do. We had to wrestle through it, and like most things in marriage, we weren't on the exact same page. I didn't want us parenting this girl. We discussed what we thought Jesus wanted us to do. More important, we agreed that the family needed to feel the weight of their own actions. We could empower them but we weren't going to keep rescuing them.

Three weeks later the mother called us. The daughter had missed the bus yet again. "I know we had a plan and we're not sticking to it," the mom said, "but could you help her out just one more time?"

This time we said sorry but no. We were not going to be the solution to their problem. Helping them this time would not provide what they truly needed, which was to come up with an answer to their problem, and it could not be us. Though we could still be friends with them, we needed to draw the line.

It made things a little awkward for a bit, but we are still friends. We have thought about the way we handled this situation. It was a tough call for us at the time, but we think we made the right decision. We did what seemed to be best for everyone.

Was that the best way to go?

Honestly, we don't know.

That's where this good neighboring stuff becomes an art form.

The hardest part about loving others is that you can always do more. You can always give more time, energy, and money to those in need. But you can't be everything to everyone, so stop making yourself feel bad about not doing more.

The challenge is realizing that it's not about what you do, but why you do it and how you do it. At the end of the day, good neighboring must be an exercise in asking God what to do in any given situation. It's about being on our knees in prayer, asking for discernment to help in the situations that we encounter. God doesn't ask us to do everything but he does ask us to do something—which is much better than nothing.

10

The Art of Focusing

As you get to know your neighbors, you begin to recognize that you can't be everyone's best friend. And let's be honest—you don't want to be. You don't have enough time or energy to invest in every one of your neighbors equally. How should you decide with whom to spend your time? Should you keep pursuing people who seem disinterested? If there seem to be more neighbor opportunities than you have time to invest, does Jesus offer wisdom about how to focus your time and energy?

The truth is that, when we practice the art of neighboring, we just won't connect at a deep level with some people. There are a lot of reasons for this, but the bottom line is that we don't have the capacity to have deep friendships with everyone. After all, there are only twenty-four hours in a day.

And if you haven't figured this out already, not everyone has time for you. People have other priorities and other relationships. Sometimes you'll end up as one of your neighbor's closest friends; sometimes you won't.

To neighbor well, you must learn to narrow your focus. You can be friendly to everybody, but it's likely that you will be good friends with only a few. Being focused is a good thing. If done well, it will allow you to have a significant impact where you live.

Some Reasons People Don't Respond

There are a lot of reasons people might not want to spend time with you. But often a lack of interest has nothing to do with you or your approach to neighboring. So if you sense some people aren't responding the way you'd hoped, keep in mind that likely it has nothing to do with you. Remember, behind every door is a story. People may be

- *Too busy.* You may have cleared your calendar so you could be more present in your neighborhood, but they have probably not done the same thing. Different people have different priorities, and it takes effort and energy to grasp the vision of being good neighbors. It's important to remember that most of us suffer from "hurry sickness."

- *Wary of you.* It's one thing for you to overcome your fears of getting to know your neighbors. But did you ever think that they might be just as wary of you? Maybe they've had bad experiences with neighbors in the past.

Maybe they're just afraid of the unknown. Perhaps they are strong introverts. Or maybe they just want to be left alone. Whatever the reason, it's okay to give people space. Sometimes it will take time for them to warm up to you. If so, then developing a friendship may take longer than you think.

- *Already relationally full.* Some of your neighbors are already well-connected with families, their church, or with a lot of other friends. Their relational calendars are full, and they simply don't have the capacity to add other friendships.

- *In a different stage of life.* At times it can be hard for people with children to connect with people who are single or who are empty nesters. Kids are great, but people who don't have kids may not want to hang out with them all day. When you and your neighbors are in different life stages, don't force the relationship if it doesn't seem to be progressing naturally.

- *Afraid of exposure.* Some people in your neighborhood are dealing with difficult and embarrassing situations. They may have addictions that they don't want others to know about. Perhaps their kids are rebellious and out of control. Maybe they have a physical limitation that makes them feel awkward around strangers. Or possibly their marriage is so explosive they aren't sure they can keep it together in front of others. It is important to remember that there is always more going on with people than meets the eye.

Jesus's Solution

We enjoy spending time with people to whom we seem to be naturally drawn. It's nice to be around people we like, especially if they like us. But it is important to note that in his ministry, Jesus was intentional about how he spent his time. Throughout the Gospels Jesus was repeatedly focused on small groups of people so he could invest in their lives in big ways. So we see that from the multitudes, he set apart a group of seventy-two disciples and commissioned them with a specific task (see Luke 10:1–17). Of those seventy-two, he had his core group of twelve, with whom he invested the majority of his time. And then from among those twelve, he was even more intentional with three and spent the most time with them.

In Matthew 17:1–9 we read about a time when Jesus left nine of his disciples and focused primarily on Peter, James, and John. These three men alone had the privilege of ascending a high mountain with Jesus, and it was on this high mountain with him where they witnessed his transfiguration.

Similarly, we see this principle in action just prior to the crucifixion. Mark 14:32–42 notes that after spending time with the twelve disciples at the Last Supper, Jesus left with them and crossed the Kidron Valley. He told his disciples to sit and wait for him while he went to pray. However, he asked Peter, James, and John to accompany him as he prayed in great distress in the Garden of Gethsemane. Clearly he felt a deeper connection with these three than with the other nine.

How do you discern the people with whom you should spend the majority of your time? It all begins with a strategic framework. Start by reaching out and becoming acquainted with everyone in your neighborhood. Learn names. Throw a block party. Invite people into your home. Then be intentional about where you spend your time. Remember, Jesus was constantly surrounded by crowds of people but was intentional with his time. He focused on a few people with most of his relational time. He didn't invest his energy in everyone equally.

A Person of Peace

When Jesus sent out the seventy-two, he gave them instructions that offer us insight into how we can best engage our neighbors. The seventy-two were called to teach, pray, and serve, and were given specific instructions on how they were supposed to do so. Jesus didn't just send them out and say, "Go and make a difference in people's lives." Instead he challenged them to look for something specific in those they met. Jesus instructed them to find a certain type of person in every city they entered—a person of peace (Luke 10:5–6). You may wonder what this has to do with neighboring.

The term *person of peace* refers to someone hospitable and open to becoming a friend. Once the disciples found a person of peace, Jesus told his followers to stay with that person. He told them specifically not to move around. At first glance, this seems odd. Shouldn't the disciples have moved around as much as possible? Wouldn't it have been best for them to stay with several different people throughout the towns? Certainly this would have allowed them to have a wider impact.

But this was not the path Jesus chose for the seventy-two. Instead, his desire was for them to set up camp in one spot, specifically in a house where the owner welcomed them. This allowed the disciples an opportunity to form deep friendships with those who were gifted at relationships themselves. Not only did they connect with the host of each house, but undoubtedly they were also introduced to the host's entire network of friends. If a person of peace was someone skilled at being hospitable, then logically they were people who would have very large networks. By directing his disciples to look for the person of peace, Jesus directed them toward those in each city who were the best neighbors.

As we get to know the people who live nearest to us, we should focus on those who can work with us to create the kind of neighboring relationships we know God desires for our neighborhood. Can you think of someone on your block you know to be very hospitable? Is there a name that popped into your mind right away? If so, odds are this is a person of peace in your neighborhood. If you cannot currently identify someone like that in your neighborhood, we encourage you to ask God to direct you to such a person.

You may wonder how to recognize a person of peace. Pay attention and you will notice the neighbors who tend to have people over a lot, maybe for a sporting event or for holiday celebrations. Look for the people who always display the best Halloween decorations or go crazy for Christmas lights. Odds are these are the people who have a desire to be connected with their neighbors. They just might be people of peace.

Bob and Mary have a story about discovering that person of peace. Bob tells it: "When we moved into our house, we were excited about learning how to be great neighbors. We had heard about the neighboring initiative at church and knew that because we were new to the block, we had a great opportunity. Honestly, we hadn't done that great a job in our old neighborhood. We felt weird about engaging our neighbors that we had lived next to for ten years. But our new surroundings created a chance for us to do things differently. Even before we made the move, we were gearing up for meeting new people.

"The day we moved in, we noticed a party going on across the street. We walked over and discovered that our new neighbors had a karaoke bar in their garage. It was complete with televisions, beer on tap, an actual bar, and a poker table. There were fifty-plus people mingling in the garage and on their driveway. At that moment it dawned on us that we probably shouldn't be the ones hosting the block party. I wouldn't even know where to buy a bar, and I certainly don't know how a keg works.

"As we got to know our neighbors, it was clear that the parties they threw didn't include the rest of the block. They simply invited their friends and hadn't ever thought to invite the neighborhood. As we shared our heart for our neighborhood, they caught the vision. They weren't the churchgoing types but could see the value of knowing and trusting their neighbors.

"Together we planned a huge block party. We even invited a live band. A few others joined in, and we had an amazing time. The cops did pay us a visit but left because there weren't any complaints. That's because all the neighbors were at the party!

"My wife and I could never have hosted a party of that magnitude. Our neighbors were simply better at throwing parties than we were. But we helped shape a vision for inviting the neighborhood to the table. Their talents mixed with our vision meant the results have been incredible. Through the process we have become great friends, and recently they even offered to host a Bible study. That's going to be one fun Bible study!"

You might not have a karaoke bar across the street, but there is someone in your neighborhood with the gift of hospitality. You just have to have eyes to see them. Focus on people of peace, and work together for the good of your neighborhood.

Investing Wisely

When Lauren and I (Dave) moved into our first neighborhood, we met a couple that we enjoyed, even though they were empty nesters. For some reason, I had the image of their being able to hang out with our kids and almost be like grandparents to them. As it turned out, they weren't very interested in being around our kids. They were really nice people, but after trying to engage them on several occasions, it soon became clear that they were enjoying the fact that their kids were gone. From what I could tell, they had paid their dues and were ready to move on.

I'd love to be able to tell you a great story about reaching out to these people and how we were able to forge a deep intergenerational, mentoring kind of relationship. But that simply didn't happen. Finally, we had to make a choice be-tween continuing to pursue a relationship with them or one with another family on our block. We chose the latter. It's not that we ignored the older couple. We've remained friendly with them but never connected deeply. And we learned to be at peace with that.

Danielle and I (Jay) encountered some of those same dy-namics a short time after moving into our neighborhood a number of years ago. We met the couple that lives catty-corner from us and liked them right off the bat. I'll call them the Parkers, though that's not really their name. Right away, we set out to be good neighbors to them.

The Parkers were young, lots of fun, and had kids about the same ages as ours. We invited them over to dinner a few times, and every time they came over, we enjoyed their com-pany. The conversation was awesome. The jokes were awe-some. The Parkers were awesome. Our friendship with them was awesome.

At least, *I* thought so.

But, strangely enough, the more we got to know the Park-ers and the more we kept inviting them to do things with us, we noticed a recurring pattern. We always did the inviting. Never them. Always us.

I'm not saying I was closely keeping track of who invited whom to do what. In fact it was Danielle who noticed that something was off. One Friday after work, we were all set to fire up the grill for dinner. "Hey," I announced, "we should invite the Parkers to come over and join us."

"You know, Jay, maybe we shouldn't this time," Danielle said.

"But why not?" I asked. Deep down I knew they were really going to like us once they got to know us.

"Well, maybe they don't want to come over."

"What are you talking about?" You could practically hear my ego being crushed.

"Well . . ." Danielle said. And then came those fateful words, "I just don't think they're that interested."

It was the same feeling I had in junior high when I found out that the girl I liked didn't feel the same. That day I began to realize an important truth about good neighboring. It's important to invest your relational time and energies wisely. If you don't, much of what you do will be in vain. That's a principle I found to be freeing. It's helped me align my priorities with God's and has helped steer my relational energy in the right direction.

The best way forward, then, is to invest time in relationships with those who seem open and responsive. When you sense that people are responding to your efforts to neighbor well, then invest time and energy in them. If they don't, be secure enough to move on.

Being Discerning

I admit it was hard for me at first to come to grips with the fact that the Parkers didn't want to be close friends with us. I strongly believed in the process of good neighboring, and we were putting effort into reaching out to them. It seemed like a natural fit for them to be good friends with us. What went wrong? Was it us? Was it them? Maybe they didn't like my sense of humor. Maybe I had a piece of spinach stuck between my teeth the last time we got together. Maybe they just didn't enjoy being with us.

As time went by, we realized that we should simply invest in relationships that were working. So Danielle and I got to know some of the other neighbors around us. We hung out in their driveways, shared a few meals, and even went camping with a couple. As the months and even years went by, we ended up being acquaintances with the Parkers, but we've never been close friends with them. They were always friendly to us but never responded to any of our attempts to go deeper. And I have learned to be at peace with that.

But—and here is the big takeaway for me—other people in our neighborhood *did* want to talk to us. Others *did* want to grow closer in friendship. Other people wanted to move along that natural progression from stranger to acquaintance to relationship. Once we learned to see the natural and effective relational two-way streets that existed around us, we began to pour effort into those relationships.

We have to learn to invest our time and energy in the people who are the most receptive. Once you have developed this skill, it will serve you well in many areas of your life. It means that you consciously make room for deeper friendships by being selective about the people you go deeper with. That may sound like the old playground practice of choosing your best friends at the expense of others. But that's not what we're advocating here. As the saying goes, when we aim at everything, we often hit nothing. So the strategy is to choose a few people to give your time and energy to and then be okay with that decision.

To get started, ask yourself, *Who are the two or three households in my neighborhood with whom we really connect and who really connect with us?* By "really connect" we don't mean that the relationship is always easy. We mean that they're really open to having a relationship with you, and you with them. Identify these people and then invest in their lives.

The idea is simple: purposely limit yourself to a few close relationships. Aim for a deeper relationship with a narrowed focus. Wise relational investing does not mean going an inch deep with many. It means going deep with a few. The principle of focusing, in a nutshell, is simply this:

Be friendly with everyone and be close to a few.

11

The Art of Forgiving

In a perfect world, everybody gets along. But we live in a world where things go wrong and people disagree. One of our friends, Pete, got off to a rough start with his neighbors because of an issue that many of us have faced. The neighbor's dog was barking and barking and barking and barking. It barked during the day. It barked during the night. Pete's family felt as though the barking had come through their walls and penetrated their skin and rattled around in their brains. Pete and his wife talked about what they might do.

Throw some rat poison wrapped in hamburger over the fence. Hmm, that might be going a little too far.

Call the police. Extreme, but a genuine possibility.

Write a note. That actually seemed like a better place to start.

So Pete wrote a note. He even signed his name and left a number that the neighbor could call. But nothing changed. The dog kept barking and barking and barking.

Pete and his wife wrestled again with what they should do. They decided not to involve the police just yet. Rather, Pete would go over and talk to the neighbor.

So Pete and the neighbor talked, but the talk didn't go well. The neighbor became defensive. Pete became defensive. And basically they agreed to disagree. The issue still wasn't resolved.

Pete knew he should be a good neighbor to this person. In fact, he *wanted* to be a good neighbor. He just didn't know how, particularly with this issue of the barking dog unresolved.

When Neighbors Are Enemies

What do you do when you have a neighbor you can't seem to get along with? Regardless of who your neighbor is or how bad a human being you think he is, you're called to love that person. You might not be called to be best friends with him. But if the person lives near you, you are called to be a good neighbor. Believe it or not, when friction exists, great opportunities exist as well.

Conflicts between neighbors are nothing new. Put any two people near each other, and they're bound to disagree over something. Maybe their tree grew too big, and now it sheds leaves all over your yard. Or maybe your neighbor leaves his windows open while playing loud music. Or perhaps your kids used to play together but they got into a squabble and now they don't hang out anymore. When you think about all the neighbors on your block, there's a good chance that you don't get along with at least one of them. Maybe more.

At first, it might seem that the easy solution would be simply to ignore the neighbor you don't get along with or to pretend the issue doesn't exist. But that strategy will only mask the problem. And if a neighbor is openly antagonistic toward you, then it's much harder to ignore the person. If you need your neighbor to interact with you to solve a problem, ignoring her won't work. The issue between you will remain.

The real solution takes us back to the Great Commandment, which of course, as we've clearly demonstrated, is still relevant for us today. Jesus has instructed us to love our neighbors, all of them. He says this is actually the best way to live. In fact, in Luke 10 he says this is the key to truly living. To do this, it's important for each of us to examine those neighboring relationships that are strained and look for ways to heal them.

Some problems with neighbors are inconsequential. They truly are. They are minor annoyances that can be overlooked with a chuckle and a bit of grace. These are problems that don't really affect anyone. They're just quirks or minor inconveniences. Perhaps your neighbor across the street gardens in the front yard with his shirt off. He is not in great shape, and you can see way too much. You know what we mean. It might be unappealing, sure. But in the grand scheme of things, it really isn't that important. In such instances you may simply need to take a step back and realize that the core issue isn't that big a deal. Back off a little bit and be more flexible.

Other problems are more middle-of-the-road. The problem of a constantly barking dog doesn't seem like a big deal compared to living next to a drug dealer with a steady stream of traffic day and night. But on a practical level, it's an issue that often needs to be addressed. This is a real problem that should be addressed, but it isn't catastrophic.

Truly catastrophic situations that arise with neighbors demand resolution. You might live close to someone who's dangerous, defiant, abusive, and uncontrollable—a truly rotten person and a real threat to the neighborhood. Then the origin of your problems is your neighbor, and you need to take steps to protect your family and the neighborhood. In such a case, you should not try to handle the problem by yourself but refer it to the proper authorities.

Excusing versus Forgiving

Most of us have problems in our neighborhoods that are in the barking dog category. When Pete, his wife, and their newborn found that they were living next to a living, breathing noise machine, they tried to find a solution. But their attempts to be good neighbors were met with resistance. The man next door didn't seem to care that his dog's barking was affecting the general peace of the neighborhood. So what was Pete supposed to do?

It might sound funny, but the realization that a problem exists is actually the beginning of the solution. Often the first step is to acknowledge that there is a problem that needs to be addressed. It's too easy to downplay such concerns, and, even though something is truly wrong, we force a smile and say, "Aw, it's okay. Everything's fine." When actually that's a lie. Things are not fine. If someone is in the wrong, God doesn't ask us to ignore the offense. What he asks us to do is forgive. Those who follow Jesus have only one choice in response to being offended: forgive. Obviously this is a lot easier said than done.

Many well-intentioned followers of Jesus think that forgiving comes in the form of ignoring. "Pretend it didn't happen," they'll say. Or, "They probably didn't mean it." This is simply a cheap way of excusing someone's bad behavior. And while doing so might make you feel like a bigger, more spiritual person, in truth you are not. This way of responding or talking falls way short of the high standard that Jesus sets for forgiveness. To forgive someone goes far beyond just excusing their behavior and moving on.

C. S. Lewis describes the difference between excusing and forgiving very eloquently:

> I find that when I think I am asking God to forgive me I am often . . . asking Him to do something quite different. I am asking Him not to forgive me but to excuse me. But there is all the difference in the world between forgiving and excusing. Forgiveness says, "Yes, you have done this thing, but I accept your apology; I will never hold it against you and everything between us will be exactly as it was before." But excusing says, "I see that you couldn't help it or didn't mean it; you weren't really to blame." If one was not really to blame then there is nothing to forgive. . . . What we call "asking God's forgiveness" very often really consists in asking God to accept our excuses.

To excuse what can really produce good excuses is not Christian charity; it is only fairness. To be a Christian means to forgive the inexcusable, because God has forgiven the inexcusable in you.[5]

So in the case of Pete and the barking dog, the answer is not for him to gloss over the issue or to try to convince himself that it's really no big deal or that God would want him to say, "Everything's fine." That would be simply excusing not forgiving.

Pete needs to be in a place where he's aware of how much he has been forgiven before he can really forgive his neighbor. He needs to have a heart that is saturated by grace if he is going to decide to forgive and honor the life he has with Jesus.

So how does that work in real life? As we've seen, neighborhood problems come in degrees of severity, so it's important to discern the reality of each situation. If a problem exists between you and a neighbor, start by asking yourself how severe it is. If it is trivial in the grand scheme of things, and you decide that it is you who needs to change, then there is no need to even bring it up to your neighbor. It might be somewhat annoying, but for the sake of being good neighbors and keeping the peace, you should overlook the issue.

When a problem is bigger, you may need to take action by having a conversation with your neighbor. And sometimes a problem might be so severe that you need to get the authorities involved.

Regardless, in all these circumstances, we are called to forgive. Whether the offense is big or small, it's vital that we do the hard work of genuinely forgiving—not just excusing.

At Peace with Everyone

The Bible's got a lot to say about being good neighbors, even when you don't get along with all of them. Romans 12:18 is a good place to start. "If it is possible, as far as it depends on you, live at peace with everyone."

If at all possible, we are to live at peace with everyone. Are we doing this? When we look around at our neighbors—even the ones who annoy us—are we doing everything we can do to get along with them? When we examine this text further, we see that living at peace with others means that we are to seek to bless them, even when they have cursed us. Here's how Paul wraps up the twelfth chapter of Romans:

> Do not repay anyone evil for evil. Be careful to do what is right in the eyes of everyone. If it is possible, as far as it depends on you, live at peace with everyone. Do not take revenge, my dear friends, but leave room for God's wrath, for it is written: "It is mine to avenge; I will repay," says the Lord. On the contrary:
>
> "If your enemy is hungry, feed him;
> if he is thirsty, give him something to drink.
> In doing this, you will heap burning coals on his head."
>
> Do not be overcome by evil, but overcome evil with good. (vv. 17–21)

Paul is saying that we should seek to bless those who have hurt us. When he talks about "heaping coals," he isn't encouraging us to burn those who have wronged us. He is using a metaphor that means people will become aware of their error because we have acted in love and have let the error stand "as is" without trying to excuse it away. Paul advocates blessing people in ways that are actual, physical, and purposeful. We need to trust that God will repay us for what has been taken from us. We also need to choose to forgive those who have hurt us. In the process, we are changed.

Matthew 5:44 takes the principle even further. Jesus says, "You have heard that it was said, 'Love your neighbor and hate your enemy.' But I tell you, love your enemies and pray for those who persecute you." This is radical teaching. Love your enemies. Pray for the neighbors you don't get along with.

The definition of an enemy is forever changed by the New Testament. Jesus takes the idea of an enemy and flips it on its head. We have to bless those who hate us. Because of what Jesus has done, everything changes.

That means when it comes to following Jesus, forgiveness is not optional. If someone wrongs us, if a neighbor annoys us, it's our job to forgive her. That means we consciously let her off the hook in our heart and mind. When we think of the infraction, we don't hold it against her. We don't harbor evil intentions in our heart. We don't want to get back at her. We're not going to take revenge into our own hands. We forgive because we have been forgiven. We forgive others because God has forgiven us.

How Many Times?

If we choose not to forgive, we are forgetting how much we have been forgiven. At one point in the Bible, Peter asks Jesus how many times he needs to forgive someone. Peter comes up with a number that seems extreme to him: seven. That probably sounded like a lot of forgiveness to Peter. Jesus answers him the way he answers a lot of questions, with a story. (It's commonly referred to as the story of the unmerciful servant and is found in Matthew 18:21–35.)

A servant owes his master a lot of money and can't repay it. It's more than he could ever pay back in his entire lifetime. He pleads with his master to have mercy on him, and his master does. He cancels the debt on the spot.

That same servant walks out and notices someone who owes him the equivalent of a loaf of bread. He walks over and demands that the man pay him what he is owed. This second man begs for mercy, but the one who had just been forgiven chooses to hold this man accountable for the lunch money. He has him thrown into prison.

The master hears about this and is furious. He tracks down the first servant and throws *him* into prison, holding him accountable for the original debt. The man had forgotten all he had been forgiven by demanding payment from someone else. As a result, the man loses the mercy that had been extended to him. Jesus ends with some ominous words in verses 34–35: "In anger his master handed him over to the jailers to be tortured, until he should pay back all he owed. This is how my heavenly Father will treat each of you unless you forgive your brother or sister from your heart." Jesus teaches clearly that forgiveness is not an option.

Forgiveness and Reconciliation

There is a world of difference between forgiveness and reconciliation. Just because we forgive someone doesn't mean we need to be best friends with him. Sometimes a relationship will still be broken, even if forgiveness has been granted. Reconciliation is the hard work of how we go forward together, whereas forgiveness is an attitude of the heart. We should offer everyone forgiveness, but we will not be reconciled with everyone we have wronged or who has wronged us.

To think theologically about this, God offers forgiveness to everyone through the atoning death and resurrection of Jesus. This is offered to all of us, regardless of what we have done or if we care about forgiveness. Not everyone, however, has been reconciled to God through Jesus, because that requires receiving the forgiveness of God through Jesus. We have to take reconciliation on the terms offered. We have to choose to humble our hearts and stop trying to earn our own freedom and relationship with God. We choose to accept forgiveness through the boundaries and terms offered in Jesus. So forgiveness is offered to all, but not all are reconciled.

Similarly, this is how we need to relate with our neighbors (near and far). We have hearts of forgiveness because we remember that we have been forgiven. We remember that forgiveness was given to us when we didn't deserve it. Since Jesus paid for us, we have been forgiven our debts, so we forgive our debtors.

As we forgive, we also seek reconciliation with others. But we make sure to forgive before we try to reconcile. It is tempting to rush to a solution, but forgiveness enables us to seek solutions that honor God and others. Without forgiving first, we seek solutions that will benefit us or just enable us to move on with unresolved issues looming in the background.

Reconciliation allows for boundaries to be set too. If someone's been abusive or if the police have been involved in an incident, reconciliation will be more difficult. For instance, you might be able to say from your heart, "Yes, I forgive you," but you will need to add, "but because of your history of abuse, I'm not going to let you be around my child." To be fully reconciled in such a case, there will need to be a process followed and parameters set by which trust is restored.

We need to remember that we must forgive people in our heart. We choose to bless those who curse us and pray for those who hurt us. In all circumstances, Jesus challenges us to have a heart that forgives and goes the extra mile. We aren't called just to do the right thing but to allow Jesus to change our heart in the midst of difficult circumstances. This is hard but it is the only way to live a free life and to continue to love deeply and freely.

The Miracle of Hearing Loss

Here's how the barking-dog scenario ended up for Pete and his family. Pete decided to be a good neighbor, even though he still felt he was in the right. He stopped worrying about being right and decided to try to be like Jesus. He saw an opportunity to do this on a snowy day in December.

Pete shoveled snow from his driveway and as he was finishing, he noticed that his neighbor, the one with the barking dog, hadn't yet had a chance to clear the snow from his driveway. Pete decided to be proactive and do something to help his neighbors. He saw an opportunity to show them he wasn't just the uptight guy who complained about their dog all the time. So he went over and shoveled their driveway.

Just as he was finishing, the front door opened. It was the brother of his neighbor. This man thanked Pete for what he was doing, and told him that his brother was in the hospital. He had recently been diagnosed with cancer.

"Suddenly, everything changed," Pete told us. "All of a sudden, the issue about their noisy dog didn't seem that important. It was ridiculous to imagine my wanting them to get their dog to keep quiet when my neighbor and his family were in the midst of this life-altering crisis."

Pete and his wife decided to reach out to their neighbor. A week later, once the neighbor returned from the hospital, they asked him if there was anything they could do to help. This was the beginning of a friendship that blossomed over time. They began to talk more and more, and slowly they began to trust each other.

In the spring of that year, Pete and his wife helped work in the neighbor's yard. They shared a few impromptu meals together and even took turns watching each other's children on occasion. Today they consider themselves real friends.

"Real relationships are almost always messy," Pete told us. "But if we're to love people the way Jesus commanded, we need to be willing to push through when things get complicated. Being a good neighbor isn't something that we can just check off the list. It has to become a way of life for us, and it is a primary way that God can use us."

Does the dog still bark?

"Yeah," Pete said. "But it just doesn't seem to matter as much anymore. In fact, it seems like it's just not as loud as it used to be."

When you are at odds with your neighbors, it can be a real challenge. It can be tempting to simply ignore them and try to move on. But Jesus asks us to do more. Often as we seek to love our neighbors, God changes us more than he changes them. Loving our difficult neighbors has the potential to transform us into the people God wants us to be. That is part of the genius of the Great Commandment. Living it out is not always easy, of course. But it is always worth it.

With this in mind, we suggest some steps to take when you have problems in your neighborhood.

- *Identify the issue and assess its severity.* Then begin from a posture of humility. Maybe the conflict is just as much your fault as it is your neighbor's. Ask yourself, *Is there anything I could have done differently in this situation?* Start with yourself when trying to identify the issue.

- *Choose to obey Jesus's command to pray for those who are your enemies.* Begin to pray for your neighbor's well-being. Pray that God will make a way for you to be reconciled. Pray that God will change your heart and convict you of anything you could have done differently. As you pray, think about all of the people you have hurt in the past. Think about the kind of prayers they've prayed about you that you would like God to answer.

- *If you're convicted by God of wrongdoing, look for an opportunity to apologize for your part in a matter.* A

genuine apology can be incredibly disarming and go a
long way toward restoring relationships and bringing
peace to a situation.

- *Go the extra mile.* Ask yourself what it will take to
  continue to live near your neighbor, to genuinely lean
  in and love this person unconditionally. Ask yourself:
  What's the most loving thing I can do for this person?
  And then do it.
- *Find an indirect way to bless people.* Sometimes engaging
  with a person face-to-face simply won't work. It will only
  escalate a tense situation or bring about more hostility. So
  is there a way to be a blessing to your neighbor without
  having to meet in person? Remember, you don't always
  need to resolve old wounds to be a good neighbor.

Neighboring is not always about being happy and comfortable; it's about allowing God to polish off rough edges.
Maturity happens when you put yourself in the place God
wants you. Don't run because there's adversity. Maybe God
wants to use the adversity to make you more like Jesus.

12

Better Together

If you're like us, you are clueless when it comes to classical music. Some of you are more cultured and have probably heard of Eric Whitacre. He is a world famous classical composer. We only heard about him because he gave a TED talk that someone recommended to us.

A few years ago Whitacre decided to conduct a fun little experiment. He wrote a song, posted the sheet music on his blog, and invited people around the world to sing the various harmonies of his song. The idea was for individuals everywhere to sing into a camera and post their videos to YouTube. Eric used the posts and created a master track with him conducting so everybody was joined together like an orchestra. Word caught on slowly. People sang and recorded their parts. The videos were posted. Eric hired a videographer to weave all the videos together.

The final result was staggering: one perfect song that featured a virtual choir of 185 voices from 12 countries, all flawlessly synced together. In the first two months of its release, the video received more than one million hits. Eric tried the experiment again a year later. This time more than two thousand people sang in his virtual choir, and again the final product was a masterpiece.[6]

When one unknown person sings, the results are often underwhelming. It's just one voice, one song, one location, one audience. But when many people come together and sing, particularly if all the people are all working toward the same goal, the results can be breathtaking. When a large number of people sing the same song together, that one song can captivate millions.

The same is true when it comes to neighboring. As one person, you can be a good neighbor. No doubt about that. But at the end of the day, your results will be limited. Yet if many people in your neighborhood come together, all with the same goal, the results will be exponentially greater. When multiple neighborhoods begin to work toward the same goal, cities can actually be changed. And if cities join with other cities, working toward similar outcomes, the results can be phenomenal.

Our journey began with a group of people sitting in a room asking, "What could we do together that we could never do alone?" To truly neighbor well, this is an important question that everyone should consider. If we've learned anything since our journey began years ago, it's that partnering with others makes a big difference. This is true when it comes to partnering with others in our neighborhoods, and it is true when it comes to local church partnerships as well.

At times, neighboring can be hard work. There will likely be a few days when you want to throw in the towel and go back to closing the garage door as soon as you get home every night. But when we work together with others, we have a built-in support system that's just a short walk or phone call away. Having someone to walk alongside in our neighboring efforts is crucial to success.

A Big Idea

When groups of like-minded people gather around kingdom causes, good things happen. A movement began when twenty people in one corner of the Denver metro area met to think, dream, and pray about what it might look like if congregations joined forces to serve our community. When our elected officials told us the best way we could serve our community was encouraging people to *become great neighbors*, something special began to take place.

Yes, we felt convicted and even embarrassed that we were being urged by our civic officials to obey the second half of the Great Commandment. But out of that moment, something powerful was birthed. We were reminded that Jesus has given us a strategic plan that has the potential to change lives, neighborhoods, and entire cities.

Much has occurred since that initial conversation. It started with twenty churches creating a sermon series that encouraged their people to go back to the basics and get intentional about knowing their immediate neighbors. Early on, we began to realize that this simple message had the ability to have an enormous impact. In that first year alone, more than seventeen thousand people heard the neighboring messages.

As we began to do the math, we realized the scope of what we were doing was much bigger than we'd originally envisioned. Those seventeen thousand made up about eight thousand households in our community. So if each of those households made a commitment to build relationships with the eight households nearest them, more than sixty thousand families and 180,000 individuals could be impacted (allowing for some overlap). It dawned on us that by simply encouraging people to commit to creating block maps and throwing block parties, we could affect almost two hundred thousand people right in our own backyard.

This movement has continued to grow quickly over a relatively short period of time. In the second year of offering the neighboring series, more than fifty congregations participated. And through www.artofneighboring.com, people were able to connect with like-minded neighbors who were hearing the same message in other congregations.

As pastors and civic leaders in other cities and states have caught wind of this idea, the movement has continued to spread. As the stories pour in, we are both surprised and excited about the way people are being impacted. If you take a look at the website today, you will see that there are now people all across the world who have heard this message and are taking steps to become better neighbors. And one of the by-products of this neighboring movement is that believers everywhere are becoming aware of the fact that their Church (capital C) is actually much bigger than they thought.

We are already seeing indications that good neighboring is changing our community for the better. We have received letters of encouragement from mayors, city managers, and police officers, describing how this initiative is paying dividends. Recently we received an email from our assistant city manager, Vicky Reir, the same person who had challenged us to become better neighbors. She wrote:

> Dave and Jay
>
> I've been working in the city manager's office for thirteen years. This is the first time that I can remember going through an entire winter without receiving a single request for assistance in shoveling their driveway. No one has asked for help for themselves or an aging parent, not one call. Maybe this is a coincidence, but I wonder if this is because of the neighboring movement. I guess there's no way to know for sure, but I thought you'd be encouraged.

It's difficult to quantify the results of good neighboring. What we do know is that when people get to know their neighbors, good things start happening. Real relationships are formed. And these relationships make a difference. Neighbors start to work together. They shovel driveways, get to know aging neighbors, notice strangers walking around, and help each other in a pinch. These small acts add up to something significant.

When Jesus was asked to pinpoint the most important commandment, he narrowed everything down to "Love God with your whole being and love your neighbor as yourself." In doing so, he gave us a simple plan that, if every believer actually took it at face value, would change the world.

This good neighboring thing actually works. Jesus really is a genius.

The Power of Teams

You can get started in your own neighboring effort by connecting with others on your block and beginning to neighbor well together. You might even want to share this book with a neighbor or two as you begin the journey. Initially it may seem more difficult to work with others instead of going it alone. After all, working with others can be complicated, and it isn't always as easy as working alone.

Find a Partner

But as we have mentioned, working with others is the best and smartest way to move forward. You can start small—just invite one person or one household into the process with you. And the neighbors you invite to join you don't all have to be Christians. There may be someone in your neighborhood who has a completely different spiritual orientation than you but knows way more about neighboring. Whether it's the Hindu family down the street, the agnostic couple behind you, or the friendly woman who can walk up to anyone and strike up a conversation, enlist these people to join your neighboring team. Remember, all truth is still God's truth, and God will honor the actions of anyone who is trying to be a good neighbor. This, after all, aligns with God's purposes.

It can be discouraging to try to draw the neighborhood together, but if just one other person is committed to the process, you won't feel so alone. At least one other person will be there when you throw a block party. You can encourage each other if you feel like you're constantly reaching out to others and getting no response.

Don't tell yourself you're too busy or too shy or don't know where to start. Just identify a neighbor you think would be a good partner and ask him or her to join you in this neighboring journey.

Using Your Gifts

Maybe you've tried in the past to be a good neighbor, and it hasn't gone according to plan. Not everyone is a naturally social person. You're just as content staying home as you are reaching out to others. At the same time you want to obey Jesus and follow him wholeheartedly. You believe in the power of the Great Commandment, and you want to neighbor well. So what do you do?

This is where working with others really pays off. Maybe your strength is simply manning the grill. You couldn't bear the thought of knocking on neighbors' doors and inviting them to a block party. But you could certainly set up all the logistics for the party if someone else actually invited the people. That's why working in teams is a big deal.

Or maybe you're relationally strong. Maybe you have so many close relationships that you are struggling to keep the ones with your neighbors going as deeply as you would like. Again, this is where the power of teamwork can come into play. Pull in others to have a role in helping your neighborhood come together. Let others plan the block party. You can be the one who does the inviting.

Recently a woman wrote to tell us of the effectiveness she experienced in good neighboring after she banded together with others: "Last year, after the challenge to meet our neighbors went out, three of us decided to resurrect the neighborhood picnic that had disappeared when the kids grew up and left home years before.

"Our neighborhood is experiencing a rebirth with a number of new families with young children moving in. The picnic last year was a great success, so we decided to do another one.

"This year we had families from four churches and another wonderful neighbor who put the picnic together. One crafty mom pulled little girls together for a fun session to create handmade invitations, which were then distributed personally to each neighbor.

"During the picnic, we had mini-tennis, complete with a volunteer certified instructor, and sidewalk chalk for the little kids. Due to a grant we received from our city, we were able to provide hamburgers, hot dogs, buns, and ice cream.

"Everyone brought lawn chairs and a side dish. Fifty people attended this year, and many stayed longer than last year. Neighbors are renewing old friendships and making new ones. An added plus is our getting to know the little ones in the neighborhood so we can look out for them. This initiative has been a huge blessing in our neighborhood."

A Spirit of Unity

Andrew described the spirit of unity he felt on his block when people from other churches joined together to neighbor well. He wrote: "In our neighborhood, we have two families at Faith Church, one at Spirit of Christ Church, and one at Grace Church. It certainly has been a blessing to discuss a shared-sermon series like this one on neighboring.

"Our idea involves something we have done occasionally in the past that has been a lot of fun. My wife, Gina, sewed some old fabric together to make a 'screen' that covers the entire wall of our garage, and then one of the other neighbors supplied a DVD player, projector, and sound system. We have movie nights for the neighborhood with a 'drive-in' feel.

"The families who have been part of our series are hoping to put together a schedule for our neighborhood this summer and expand the movie nights to include some grilling and eating before the movie. In the process of planning the movies for the summer, we will be able to offer a variety of shows and include a few that have a distinctly Christian message.

"For others looking for ideas, I would simply pass on that this 'drive-in' idea is really not that hard to pull off and is a lot of fun. When we have done it in the past, we get a lot of participation from many neighbors. Everyone brings a lawn chair and comes out to enjoy a nice Colorado night."

It's clear that once you begin to partner with other neighbors, you will find that the sum is far greater than the parts.

The Power of Working Together

Throughout the Gospels, Jesus teaches us that we are better when we work together. He built a team of twelve disciples. He sent people out two by two (Luke 10:1–3). In the book of Acts, we read that Paul worked with Barnabas, then later with Silas. Barnabas also worked with John Mark. And Peter worked with John. This chain of people runs right into present history. The story of God is told through the lives of people who collaborate and quite literally turn the world upside down. As we look back, we can see that God used these small groups of people literally to change the world.

Given all these good results, it seems strange that believers and churches are not better at working together. Why is it that partnerships between people of different congregations seem to be the exception and not the norm? This is a question both ministry leaders and believers need to address. For starters, we believe Christians stay apart for two reasons: we fear that unity equals uniformity and we want to focus solely on our own church.

Fear of Unity

It's important to identify what is essential and what is nonessential when it comes to partnering with others. Maybe you prefer a style of worship music that is different from that of the church across the street. You might wear jeans and T-shirts to church, while people in other churches wear suits and ties. You may baptize with a sprinkle, and others dunk people all the way.

Often Christians and churches define themselves by how they differ from one another. But we believe there's incredible power in focusing on the 98 percent on which we all agree. It's important to realize that, at the end of the day, we are on the same team. If other groups believe that Jesus is the Son of God and that he gave us the Great Commandment, then it's probably safe to partner with them when it comes to neighboring.

Focus on Our Own Church

We believe that it's vital for believers to be committed to a specific local church. This is the place where they will grow in faith, serve in ministry, and give of their resources. But as we get more and more involved in the ministry of our church, it's easy to get so wrapped up in what God is doing in our congregation that we lose sight of the big picture—God's kingdom.

Keep in mind, local churches play a very important role in God's plan to build the kingdom, but each local church is just one part of the kingdom. That's what it's all about. After all, Jesus uses the word *church* only 3 times in the Gospels; he uses the word *kingdom* 121 times.

In John 17 Jesus prays that believers everywhere would be one. He states that if we live in unity, the world around us will be drawn toward God and will begin to see that Jesus is who he says he is. Historically, churches have not always done a good job of working together. Jesus's prayer for unity means more than just believing a set of statements, it means learning to work together. This is a powerful prayer and one that we all need to spend time thinking about.

As we have been meeting with other pastors, we have been reminded that Jesus was right: unity among believers causes people who don't know God to pause and take notice. When others see us working together for the good of our communities, they get curious and begin to ask questions. This is the way Jesus always wanted it to be, and those around us are watching.

You aren't meant to do neighboring alone. As you engage in this kind of life with others, something miraculous happens. You have the ability to start a movement. You can be a part of helping bring about a transformation, not just of your block or neighborhood but of your entire city and beyond. Change happens most often with a series of small steps in the same direction. Your small voice can add to the hundreds and thousands of others in your city.

Simple but Powerful

Jesus really is a genius. He has asked us to be good neighbors, and there's a reason why: good neighboring works. It works for your neighborhood, your city, and for each of us as individuals. "'Love the Lord your God with all your heart and with all your soul and with all your strength and with all your mind'; and, 'Love your neighbor as yourself'" (Luke 10:27).

We believe strongly that too few of us actually take the Great Commandment literally. But what would it be like to actually love our neighbors—our actual neighbors, the people who live no less than thirty feet from us? Imagine if every Christian interpreted what Jesus said as the most important thing to do and actually did it. Imagine if every person made decisions about their schedules to make good neighboring a priority. There's so much potential in this movement. The world really could be changed.

Good neighboring does not involve any huge complicated plan. It just involves taking small steps to move from stranger to acquaintance to relationship. If you encounter people who aren't interested, that's okay. Just look for people who are, because, at its core, that's really all the art of neighboring is about. It's simple but it's also very powerful.

The wonder is that people from so many diverse backgrounds see the power in neighboring well. We've talked to police chiefs, housing managers, city leaders, pastors, teachers, city strategists, and plenty of plain old neighbors like you and us—and everybody gets it. When people reach out to other people in kind ways, good things happen.

Let's take a moment to revisit the block map. It's not meant to shame anyone. Remember, conviction is not the same thing as shame. The point of the exercise is to take the invitation to love our neighbors from theory to practice. The exercise is a tool designed to help us see the reality of our lives.

You filled out the block map at the start of this book. Now, however long it's been since you started reading this book, let's see how much progress has been made.

Again, imagine that the boxes on page 183 are the eight houses situated closest to you. Each of the eight boxes represent the eight houses or apartments closest to yours. In the box in the middle, write your home address. In the other boxes, fill in the three subpoints within each box—a, b, and c—as directed below.

- a—Write down the names of the people who live in the house represented by the box. If you can give first and last names, that's great. If it's only first names, that's fine too.
- b—Write down some relevant information about each person, some data or facts about him or her that you

couldn't see just by standing in your driveway, things you might know if you've spoken to the person once or twice.

- c—Write down some in-depth information you would know after connecting with people. This might include their career plans or dreams of starting a family or anything to do with the purpose of their lives. Write down anything meaningful that you know about them.

Okay, how did you do? Were you able to fill out more of the chart than you could when you started reading this book? If you haven't made any progress on your block map, then we want to encourage you to start small but start today. Make it a priority to fill in at least one new name this week. If you don't feel that you have the time to do this, then take out your calendar and answer this question: Is everything that I am currently doing more important than taking the Great Commandment literally?

If you have made some progress on your block map, then be encouraged. Continue looking, continue praying, continue asking God to open up doors and move you down the line with your neighbors from stranger to acquaintance to relationship. Again, the small steps count. If you have recently met a neighbor and learned his or her name, then you are well on your way.

And remember, this is a journey that doesn't end. That's the beauty of the art of neighboring. Don't let your desire and passion for neighboring fade away. If God has spoken to you as you have read this book, then we want to encourage you to step out and make a difference in your neighborhood. We all have

a.

b.

c.

a.

b.

c.

a.

b.

c.

a.

b.

c.

a.

b.

c.

a.

b.

c.

a.

b.

c.

a.

b.

c.

gifts and talents that can be used for something significant in our neighborhoods, something that really matters. And good neighboring matters.

Whoever you are, whatever your personality, you can do this. When the people who live around each other become closer in their relationships, great things happen. We believe that neighboring is the answer to solving the biggest social issues that exist in our communities today. It works better than any program, and it works better than any government initiative.

Start now, start by doing the small things well, and commit to good neighboring as a lifestyle. You have been invited to begin a sacred journey, one that has the potential to change your block, your city, and possibly the world.

Study Guide

We have included this study guide to help you enter into meaningful conversation with others who have a desire to grow as believers and neighbors. We believe that the best way to learn about neighboring is in the context of community. Ideally, you will be able to process the principles found in this book with a group of your friends. The following questions will provide a loose framework for your discussions. We encourage you to chase rabbit trails, welcome tangents, and be open to where God leads your conversations. Each session covers two chapters and is designed to be used after the corresponding material has been read.

SESSION 1
THE CALL TO NEIGHBORING

CHAPTERS 1 & 2

Starter Question: What factors did you consider before choosing your current residence?

Read Acts 17:26–27

What do you like about this passage? Do you have any questions about these verses?

Reflection/Discussion Questions

1. How much of your block map were you able to fill in? Did you have any epiphanies as you did this exercise?

2. Describe your neighborhood and the relationships that you currently have with your immediate neighbors. Do you have any invisible neighbors?

3. According to Acts 17:26–27, why do we live where we live? And why has God placed us in our neighborhoods?

4. In chapter one the mayor states; "The majority of the issues that our community is facing would be eliminated or drastically reduced if *we could just figure out a way to become a community of great neighbors.*" To what extent do you think this is true?

5. Luke 10:29 says this about the teacher of the law: "But he wanted to justify himself, so he asked Jesus, 'And who is my neighbor?'" In what ways do we attempt to justify ourselves in order to avoid taking the Great Commandment seriously?

6. What would happen if every Christ-follower made it a point to know and befriend their literal neighbors?

Action Steps

1. Create your own block map and place it somewhere in your home where you will see it often.

2. Learn the name of one of your unknown neighbors this week and fill in their squares on your block map.

Session 2
Overcoming Barriers

Chapters 3 & 4

Starter Question: On a scale of 1 to 10, how hectic is life right now?

Read Luke 10:38–42

What do you like about this passage? Do you have any questions about these verses?

Reflection/Discussion Questions
1. Which of the following myths do you struggle with the most?
   a. Things will settle down someday.
   b. More will be enough.
   c. Everybody lives like this.
      What practical steps can you take in order to break the habit of thinking like this?

2. Do you currently live at a pace that allows you to be present in your neighborhood?

3. Are there some good things in your life that are keeping you from the "main thing"?

4. Discuss the impact that technology has had on how you view the world.

5. Are you skeptical about anyone on your block? Why?

6. Discuss or think about some practical ways you can overcome your fears of interacting with neighbors you don't know.

Action Steps

1. Look at your calendar and do an audit of how you have spent your time over the last two weeks. Reflect on how well your calendar is aligned with your priorities.

2. Go and meet one of your neighbors who you know nothing about. Leave a note if they don't come to the door.

Session 3
Moving Down the Line

Chapters 5 & 6

Starter Question: What is the best party that you have ever been to?

Read Luke 5:27–32

What do you like about this passage? Do you have any questions about these verses?

Reflection/Discussion Questions

1. In what ways did Jesus's behavior at the party challenge the social norms of his day?

2. What would it cost you to participate in or organize the kind of parties Jesus was known to attend?

3. Who currently throws the best parties in your neighborhood?

4. Take out your block map and identify which of the following three words best describes each of your eight closest neighbors—Stranger, Acquaintance, or Relationship?

5. Share something that you have done for or with someone that seemed small at the time but had a big impact.

6. What are the activities you most enjoy doing, and how might they become tools for building relationships with your neighbors?

Action Steps

1. Partner with someone on your block and begin to plan a neighborhood block party.

2. Be purposeful this week in doing one small thing that moves you down the line:
Stranger→Acquaintance→Relationship

SESSION 4
POSTURE IS EVERYTHING

CHAPTERS 7 & 8

Starter Question: When was the last time you had a conversation with someone who seemed to have an ulterior motive?

Read Matthew 5:14–16
What do you like about this passage? Do you have any questions about these verses?

Reflection/Discussion Questions
1. Has anyone ever tried to sell you something that you weren't interested in?

2. Why do some people have a lot of baggage when it comes to having spiritual conversations?

3. Are you comfortable sharing your story and telling people about the impact Jesus has on your life? When did you last share your story with someone?

4. "We don't love our neighbors to convert them; we love our neighbors because we are converted" (p. 102). Discuss the tension in this statement.

5. Are you good at allowing other people to care for you?

6. "The art of receiving is not complicated. It comes down to being aware of our own needs. It's about opening our eyes, then being vulnerable enough to ask and receive" (p. 128). What current needs do you have that a neighbor might be able to help you with?

Action Steps

1. Try telling a friend your whole story as it relates to God. Ask them for feedback.

2. Ask someone in your neighborhood for help or advice in an area where you are lacking.

Session 5
Open Doors

Starter Question: Share about a time in your life when God guided you by opening or closing a door.

Read Matthew 17:1–9

What do you like about this passage? Do you have any questions about these verses?

Reflection/Discussion Questions

1. How would you have felt if you were one of the nine disciples who weren't invited by Jesus to go up on the mountain?

2. Why do you think that Jesus made a decision to spend the majority of his time with a small group of people?

3. What's the difference between being responsible *to* a person and being responsible *for* a person?

4. Have you ever encountered a "messy" situation in neighboring? What happened?

5. Have you ever had a friendship in which you felt that no matter what you did, it was never enough? Share about this experience.

6. Which of your neighbors do you feel God calling you to spend more time with?

Action Steps

1. Reflect on Luke 10:5–11. Write down the names of the people of peace in your neighborhood.

2. Invite a neighbor over to your house for dinner.

Session 6
A United Front

Chapters 11 & 12

Starter Question: Share about a conflict that you've had with a neighbor.

Read Romans 12:14–21

What do you like about this passage? Do you have any questions about these verses?

Reflection/Discussion Questions

1. What happens over time when we fail to forgive people who have wronged us?

2. Have you ever become acquaintances or friends with someone who you once considered an enemy?

3. Share about a time in which you worked with others to accomplish something significant.

4. What are some of the reasons Christ-followers refuse to work together? How valid are these reasons?

5. What would your city be like if every Christian made a decision to become a better neighbor?

Action Steps

1. Walk around your block and ask God to give you a vision for what he wants your neighborhood to look like.

2. Share your neighboring stories with others. Encourage some of your friends to take the Great Commandment seriously and reach out to their neighbors.

Notes

1. John Ortberg, from a sermon preached at Willow Creek in 2000.

2. Malcolm Gladwell, *Outliers* (New York: Little, Brown, 2008), 40.

3. Ortberg, *The Life You've Always Wanted* (Grand Rapids: Zondervan, 2002), 87.

4. Henry Cloud and John Townsend, *Boundaries* (Grand Rapids: Zondervan, 2002), 29.

5. C. S. Lewis, "On Forgiveness" in *The Weight of Glory and Other Addresses,* rev. and exp. ed. (1947; New York: Macmillan, 1980), 122–25.

6. See the TED talk that described Eric Whitacre's process at: http://www.ted.com/talks/view/lang/eng//id/1110.

Recommended Resources

We have been greatly influenced by many different leaders. This is a list of many of the resources that have shaped our thinking. We are grateful to all of the leaders mentioned below and many that we haven't listed here.

Chapter 1

The Abundant Community, John McKnight and Peter Block

Building Communities from the Inside Out, John P. Kretzmann and John L. McKnight

Holding Ground, a video by New Day Films, http://www.newday.com/films/Holding_Ground.html

Putting Faith in Neighborhoods, Stephen Goldsmith

Chapter 2

Outliers, Malcolm Gladwell
The Connecting Church, Randy Frazee
Life Together, Dietrich Bonhoeffer
Radical, David Platt

Chapter 3

Making Room for Life, Randy Frazee
The Life You've Always Wanted, John Ortberg
Taking It to the Limit: Sermon series by Andy Stanley from North-
    point Community Church, http://store.northpoint.org/take-it-to-
    the-limit-1.html
The Power of Full Engagement, Jim Loehr and Tony Schwartz
The 4-Hour Workweek, Timothy Ferriss
The One Minute Manager, Kenneth H. Blanchard and Spencer Johnson
"How to Make Work-Life Balance Work," TED talk by Nigel Marsh,
    http://www.ted.com/talks/nigel_marsh_how_to_make_work_life_
    balance_work.html

Chapter 4

Crazy Love, Francis Chan
Chasing Daylight, Erwin Raphael McManus
Bowling Alone, Robert D. Putnam
Fearless, Max Lucado
A Failure of Nerve, Edwin H. Friedman

Chapter 5

Edmonton Block Party Kit, http://www.edmonton.ca/for_residents/
    Block-Party-Guide.pdf

Good Magazine, *The Neighborhoods Issue*, http://www.good.is/series/
neighborhoods-issue

The Tangible Kingdom, Hugh Halter and Matt Smay

"5 Ways to Listen Better," TED talk by Julian Treasure, http://www.
ted.com/talks/julian_treasure_5_ways_to_listen_better.html

Chapter 6

The Rise of Christianity, Rodney Stark

Just Walk Across the Room, Bill Hybels

"How to Start a Movement," TED talk by Derek Sivers, http://www.
ted.com/talks/derek_sivers_how_to_start_a_movement.html

Chapter 7

The Divine Conspiracy, Dallas Willard

To Transform a City, Eric Swanson and Sam Williams

Mere Christianity, C. S. Lewis

Speaking of Jesus, Carl Medearis

A Million Miles in a Thousand Years, Donald Miller

Chapter 8

Compassion, Justice and the Christian Life, Robert D. Lupton

Irresistible Revolution, Shane Claiborne

"The Power of Vulnerability," TED talk by Brene Brown, http://www.
ted.com/talks/brene_brown_on_vulnerability.html

Chapter 9

Boundaries, Henry Cloud and John Townsend

Codependent No More, Melody Beattie

When Helping Hurts, Steve Corbett and Brian Fikkert

Chapter 10

The Master Plan of Evangelism, Robert E. Coleman
"Born to Reproduce," Dawson Trotman, http://www.discipleshiplibrary.com
Focus, Leo Babauta
The Sacred Echo, Margaret Feinberg

Chapter 11

Total Forgiveness, R. T. Kendall
Free of Charge, Miroslav Volf
What's So Amazing about Grace?, Philip Yancey
The Weight of Glory, C. S. Lewis

Chapter 12

Breaking the Missional Code, Ed Stetzer and David Putman
The Tipping Point, Malcolm Gladwell
"A Tale of Two Cities," Sermon by Timothy Keller, http://sermons2.redeemer.com/sermons/sermonlist/11
A Theology as Big as the City, Ray Bakke
The Starfish and the Spider, Ori Brafman and Rod A. Beckstrom

Jay Pathak is the lead pastor of Mile High Vineyard Church, which has campuses in Arvada and Denver, Colorado. Prior to planting Mile High in 2001, Jay served at the Columbus Vineyard and was one of the leaders in its young-adult ministry, Joshua House. Additionally, he served as an intern to the senior pastor, Rich Nathan. Jay is a graduate of Ohio State University with a BA in philosophy and a graduate of the Vineyard Leadership Institute. He has spoken nationally and internationally for the Vineyard and other groups in both conference and classroom settings. Currently he serves on the National Board of Vineyard USA. Jay and his wife, Danielle, have two daughters.

Dave Runyon helps faith, business, and government leaders work together in the Denver Metro area. He serves as the executive director of CityUnite and as a consultant for companies that have a desire to make a positive impact in their communities (cityunite.org). Previously, Dave served as a pastor for nine years at Foothills Community Church and The Next Level Church. In 2010 he led a neighboring movement that mobilized over 70 churches and 40,000 people in the Denver Metro area. He graduated from Colorado State University, where he studied history and secondary education. He speaks locally and nationally encouraging leaders to collaborate for the good of their cities. Dave and his wife, Lauren, have four kids and do not plan to have any more.

Come, join the good neighboring movement:
www.artofneighboring.com